GOD AND EVIL

God and Evil
The Problem Solved

Gordon Haddon Clark

The Trinity Foundation

God and Evil: The Problem Solved
Chapter 5 of *Religion, Reason and Revelation*
Copyright © 1961
Lois A. Zeller and Elizabeth Clark George

This edition copyright © 2004 John W. Robbins
Published by
The Trinity Foundation
Post Office Box 68
Unicoi, Tennessee 37692
www.trinityfoundation.org

ISBN: 1-940931-73-7

Contents

FOREWORD 7

GOD AND EVIL
Historical Exposition 9
Free Will 12
Reformation Theology 17
Gill's Exegesis 23
Omniscience 25
Responsibility and Free Will 26
The Will of God 27
Puppets 28
Appeal to Ignorance 32
Responsibility and Determinism 33
Distortions and Cautions 35
Deo Soli Gloria 41

SCRIPTURE INDEX 42
INDEX 43
THE CRISIS OF OUR TIME 49

Foreword

ONE OF the perennial objections to Christianity is the problem of evil.

The problem may be stated as follows: If God is all-good, and if God is all-powerful, why are sin and suffering in the world? Surely if God were both all-good and all-powerful, he would rid the world of evil, or, better yet, would not have allowed sin and suffering to appear in the first place. But since evil does exist, it must be that

(1) God is not all-good, even though he is almighty, and so he does not wish to end sin and suffering; or
(2) God is all-good, but not almighty, and so he cannot rid the world of sin and suffering, no matter how good he is; or
(3) God is neither all-good nor all-powerful, and so neither wishes to, nor can, rid the world of evil; or
(4) there is no God at all; or
(5) there is more than one god, none of whom is omnipotent, and one or more of whom may be evil; or
(6) god is impersonal, and the ascription of intelligence or purposes to it is a pathetic fallacy.

Whichever alternative is chosen, the existence of the God of the Bible is disproved (so the argument goes), for the Bible speaks of one God who is both good and all-powerful.

Theologians have attempted to answer this argument for centuries. They have offered two major counter-arguments: First, they have denied the existence of sin and suffering, which, of course, contradicts the Bible. Second, they have asserted that man has free will, which also contradicts the Bible. The free-will argument has been the most popular proposed solution to the problem of evil, but it actually seeks to solve the problem by agreeing to one of the problem's alternatives: The free-will argument concedes that God is not almighty, for the free will of man can and does frustrate God's will. The free-will argument is really a capitulation to and an agreement with the unbeliever, for, like the unbeliever, the defender of free will is left with a god who may

The problem may be stated as follows: If God is all-good, and if God is all-powerful, why are sin and suffering in the world?

be good, but who is not omnipotent, and therefore he is not and cannot be the God of the Bible.

Now there is a solution to the problem of evil, and it has been staring theologians in the face for millennia. Almost all of them have been blind to it. The solution is found in the Scriptures themselves, in the very description of God that the unbeliever twists into an argument against God. Dr. Clark set forth that solution in a British journal in 1932 when he was 29 years old, and then he published it again 30 years later in his book, *Religion, Reason, and Revelation*, from which this essay is taken.

It is only in the Scriptures that the solution to the problem of evil is found. No other proposed solution solves the problem of evil. Counterfeit Christianities, such as Arminianism and Romanism, cannot solve the problem; in fact, the problem of evil proves those counterfeits to be false. Their proponents do not understand the sovereignty of God, nor the origin of moral law, including the concepts of good and evil, nor the basis for human responsibility. Consequently, the unbeliever, wielding the problem of evil as his weapon, has slain Arminianism and Romanism.

But the problem of evil has no force against Biblical Christianity, which denies assumptions on which the argument is founded: (1) that the concept of goodness has some meaning apart from God and is somehow superior to God; (2) that God is benevolent toward all his creatures; and (3) that God's actions are not by definition just, righteous, and good. Once one understands the Biblical doctrine of God, the problem of evil is properly seen as an argument that slays lesser gods, counterfeit gods, but cannot even bruise the God of the Bible.

John W. Robbins

God and Evil

In the background of every religious worldview there stands a frightening spectre. An author may refrain from mentioning it; he may hope that his public will forget to think about it; but no position is complete and none can be unhesitatingly accepted until it makes a clear pronouncement on the problem of evil.

> Of man's first disobedience, and the fruit
> Of that forbidden tree whose mortal taste
> Brought Death into the world, and all our woe....
> Sing heavenly muse....[1]

It is not, however, the sonorous phrases of a great poet nor even the inspiration of a Muse that we need. Careful thought, cleancut definitions, and consistency to the end are the prerequisites of progress. The aim of this chapter is to face the question of evil squarely, without dodging, and to show that, whereas various other views disintegrate at this point, the system known as Calvinism and expressed in the *Westminster Confession of Faith* offers a satisfactory and completely logical answer.

Historical Exposition

To bring the matter into sharp focus and to set forth the main difficulties, a representative selection will be made from the discussions of history. In antiquity, evil was almost always viewed from the standpoint of some sort of religion; at the present time, God is more frequently left out of the picture. Although the presuppositions of this chapter are thoroughly theistic, something will be said of non-theistic views, if only to indicate that the problem of evil does not disappear with the acceptance of secularism.

The problem, as it has usually been considered, is terrifyingly simple. How can the existence of God be harmonized with the existence of evil? There are plenty of evils. One of the Soviet secret police is quoted as boasting that he had so refined torture that he could break every

> *The aim of this chapter is to face the question of evil squarely, without dodging, and to show that, whereas various other views disintegrate at this point, the system known as Calvinism and expressed in the Westminster Confession of Faith offers a satisfactory and completely logical answer.*

[1]. John Milton, *Paradise Lost*. 1-6.

bone in a man's body without killing him. And is there a God who looks down on this from on high? By those who were religiously inclined the enigma has been faced in fear and trembling; the irreligious – Voltaire, for example – with a cry of triumph have spat it forth like the poison of asps. But whatever the form, the issue is inescapable: How can the existence of God be reconciled with the existence of evil?

In early Christian times Lactantius reports its prevalence. If God is good and wants to eliminate sin, but cannot, he is not omnipotent; but if God is omnipotent and can eliminate sin, but does not, he is not good. God cannot be both omnipotent and good.

Although the Christian concept of God as omnipotent aggravates the difficulty, man's trouble with evil – his intellectual trouble with evil – did not begin with Christianity. Pain, disease, calamities, injustice, and woe have impressed people of every religion. Some religions, of which Zoroastrianism is one, concluded that the universe must be the work of two independent, conflicting deities. Neither the good god nor the evil god is omnipotent, and neither has as yet destroyed the other. On the surface, this seems to account for the mixture of good and evil in the world; but such ultimate and irreducible dualisms give rise to further riddles which many philosophers have thought equally insoluble.

Plato in his *Republic* attempted to account for evil by the assumption that God is not the cause of everything, but only of a few things – few because our evils far outnumber our goods.

In the *Timaeus* he was not quite so pessimistic, but he still held that there is an eternal and chaotic Space which the Demiurge cannot entirely control. To the end, therefore, it must be said, Plato retained an unreconciled dualism.

Aristotle, because his philosophy is so completely irreligious, is somewhat an exception in antiquity. He conceived God in such a way that his relation to evil, or to the moral endeavors of men, hardly mattered. The Unmoved Mover is in a sense the cause of all motion, but instead of being an active cause, he causes motion by being the object of the world's desire. He exercises no voluntary control over history. Though he is constantly thinking, he does not seem to think about the world, or, at most, he knows only a part of the past and nothing whatever of the future.

Naturally, the great Christian philosopher Augustine grappled with the difficulty. Under Neoplatonic influence he taught that all existing things are good; evil, therefore, does not exist – it is metaphysically unreal. Being nonexistent, it can have no cause, and God therefore is not the cause of evil. When a man sins, it is a case of his choosing a lower good instead of a higher good. This choice too has no efficient cause, although Augustine assigns to it a deficient cause. In this way God was supposed to be absolved. Augustine, admittedly, was a great Christian and a great philosopher. Later in the chapter more will be said about him. But here he was at his worst. Deficient causes, if there are such things, do not explain why a good God does not abolish sin and guarantee that men always choose the highest good.

This matter of evil is not an outmoded antiquity that evaporated with Zoroaster, Aristotle, or Augustine. The twentieth century cannot evade it. Therefore a few illustrations will be selected from contemporary writers. Today, however, much of the discussion is secular in nature. Either religion is ignored, or, in some cases, Christianity is pointedly attacked.

Lucius Garvin, John L. Mothershead, and Charles A. Baylis have each written a textbook on ethics. These books are fairly well known in American colleges today. Garvin has a very short section on theological ethics, with a conclusion that suggests that God is not particularly important; in the second textbook the index has no entry at all for God; and in the third it seems that God is mentioned on only one page. Nevertheless, secular ethics, although it will pay no attention to omnipotence, must still consider determinism and must say something about responsibility. An example of this type of thought will elucidate some details of the main argument as well as serve as part of an historical selection.

Professor Baylis of Duke University gives what many people will believe to be a very plausible argument. If determinism is true, he says, then a person's decisions reflect his character. The man's character causes and explains his actions. Accordingly, if we know the particular weaknesses of a man's character, we may be able – by praise, promises, threats, or punishments – to alter his character, improve the man, and so produce better decisions. Blame and punishment, therefore, which have the effect of reforming a person, are justifiable; but retributive punishment will not be justifiable, if determinism is true. The remote causes of a man's character are far in the past and were never under his control. Therefore he is not responsible for them, and therefore retributive punishment is illegitimate. Dr. Baylis further insists that indeterminism also renders retributive punishment illegitimate; and what is worse, indeterminism can provide only a dubious justification for corrective punishment.

Another professor at Duke University furnishes an example of those who pointedly attack Christianity. The argument comes from *An Introduction to the Philosophy of Religion*, by Dr. Robert Leet Patterson.

To refer evil to a corrupt human nature transmitted from Adam, Professor Patterson brands as "an odious doctrine which Pelagius, to his honor, anticipated modern liberals in rejecting" (218n3). Besides, there is a previous question. The author asks, "If it be as easy for God to create good men as to create evil men, why did not God create all men good?" (173). To suppose that God created the good and the evil for his own glory, to bestow his love on the good and his wrath on the evil, is to lower God to the level of the most degenerate human tyrant. Such an idea must be decisively rejected, for, the author insists (177), God cannot be thought of as immoral. Even if we believe, in the absence of all evidence, that every occurrence of evil is essential to the

> *"If it be as easy for God to create good men as to create evil men, why did not God create all men good?"*
> – R. L. Patterson

realization of a greater good, the fact that God could not produce the good without the previous evil indicates that God's power is limited (179).

Today, then, as in the past, the existence of evil is a crucial question; and the answer frequently includes the idea of a limited deity. Many modern philosophers, such as John Stuart Mill, William Pepperell Montague, and Georgia Harkness, as well as the ancient Zoroaster and Plato, accept a finite god. But it must be clearly understood that this idea is incompatible with Christianity. The Bible presents God as omnipotent, and only on this basis can a Christian view of evil be worked out.

The idea of a finite god, although it is a non-Christian expedient, has nonetheless a certain amount of merit by reason of its honesty. Professing Christians are not always so frank. In a certain Christian college the head of the Bible Department used to tell his students not to discuss the subject (indeed, this was rather clearly the policy of the institution), for the subject is controversial. It is also unedifying. And the professor should have added, it is embarrassing. For when some pointed questions were asked him, he grew irritated and replied, "I do not like the kind of questions you ask." Perhaps such colleges think that if evil is never mentioned, the students will never hear about it. They seem to forget that the secular enemies of Christianity will soon remind them and ask them controversial, unedifying, and embarrassing questions. Such an attitude of secrecy did not characterize the great Christian theologians: Augustine, Aquinas, Calvin. We may perhaps not agree with this one or that one, but like the modern secularists they were open and honest. Before we drop the idea of a finite god, however, there is one interesting consideration to mention. If the mixture of good and evil in the world rules out the possibility of a good and omnipotent God, and if the extent of good in the world hardly allows the assumption of an infinite evil demon, it still does not follow that there is a finite good God. A finite evil god is an equally acceptable conclusion. Instead of saying that God does the best he can, but being limited he cannot quite eliminate the evil in the world, we could just as well say that God does the worst he can, but being limited he cannot quite eradicate the forces of good which oppose his will. Evidently, therefore, the advocates of a finite god arrive at their conclusion more by emotion than by reason.

Free Will

Because of God's omniscience, most probably, Augustine recognized that the metaphysical unreality of evil and the supposition of deficient causes were inadequate to dispose of the difficulties. Accordingly, he added a theory of free will. From pagan antiquity, through the Middle Ages, on down into modern times, free will has doubtless been the most popular solution offered for the problem of evil. God is all-powerful, many people will say, but he has adopted a hands-off policy and allows men to act apart from divine influence. We choose, and we choose evil, of our own free wills; God does not make us do so; therefore, we alone are responsible, and not God.

This theory of free will must now be carefully examined. Is it a satisfactory theory? Do its proponents have an unambiguous concept of its chief term? Is it true that the will is free? And if it is true, does free will solve the problem of evil?

Augustine's formulation of the theory of free will, like many other of his views, did not remain unaltered. In his pagan life he had been a Manichaean; he had accepted an ultimate dualism of good and evil. After his conversion, although he had a brilliant mind, he did not immediately see the implications of the Biblical assertions so clearly as he did later in life. It took time even for Augustine to develop.

His early view of free will seems to be that all men are completely untrammeled in their decisions. Anyone can as easily choose this as that. Neither divine grace nor any other force determines a man in either direction. In his work on *Free Will,* he begins by wondering how it is possible for all souls, seeing that they commit sin, to have come from God without referring those sins back to God. In other words, if God created souls which are now sinful, is not God responsible for sin? And to go further, "I ask whether a free will itself, by which we are proved to have a power to sin, should have been given us by him who made us. For it is clear that if we were without free will we would not sin; and in this way it is to be feared that God may be adjudged the author of our evil doing" (I, ii and xvi).

To avoid this conclusion, the explanation (or at least a part of it), is that without free will we could as little do good as evil. A being, such as a stone or perhaps a bug, that cannot do evil is equally incapable of doing good. The ability to do good or evil is one, and God is not to blame if man uses his freedom wrongly. Free will may indeed do wrong, but there is no right action without it. Even sin does not justify the assertion that it were better if sinners did not exist. There must be all grades of being in the world. Variety is essential. Even a soul that perseveres in sin is better than any inanimate body that cannot sin because it has no will.

One must pause, however. From the metaphysical assumption that being is *better* than non-being, does it follow that a sinner is *better off* than a stone? What would Augustine have said if he had remembered Christ's statement, "It would have been good for that man if he had not been born"? Such questions come to mind, but the exposition of Augustine's views must continue.

So far it would seem that free will is the property of all men. The very possibility of doing either good or evil requires it. But toward the end of the book Augustine introduces a thought which he expands in his later writings. Noting that men now inevitably sin and cannot avoid it, he says, "When we speak, then, of the will free to do right, we speak of the will in which man first was made" (III, xviii). Thus it appears that no one now has a free will.

In the *City of God* (XXII, xxx), Augustine makes this point clearer.

> *"I ask whether a free will itself, by which we are proved to have a power to sin, should have been given us by him who made us. For it is clear that if we were without free will we would not sin; and in this way it is to be feared that God may be adjudged the author of our evil doing."*
> —*Augustine*

Adam had free will in the sense that he was able not to sin. This presumably is the popular notion of free will. Most people seem to mean by it that a man is just as able to will one thing as its opposite. He is free, they say, because he can choose to obey or to disobey God's commands. But by the time that Augustine wrote the *City of God* he had learned enough about the Bible, and about men too, to know that in this age it is impossible for anyone not to sin. Sin is inevitable. Therefore the ability to do good or evil is not one. Though the unregenerate do evil, they cannot do good. In the future, when our redemption shall have been completed and we are glorified in Heaven, another impossibility will appear. There we shall be unable to sin. Again the ability to do good or evil is not one, for though we shall do good, we shall not be able to do evil. There are thus three stages in the total human drama: before the fall, *posse non peccare* (possible not to sin); and in the world to come, *non posse peccare* (not possible to sin); but in this present world, *non posse non peccare* (not possible not to sin). Adam therefore was the only man who ever had free will – free will in the usual sense of the term.

The phrase *free will*, however, had such attractive connotations that Augustine did not wish to limit it to Adam. Hence he immediately continues, "Is God himself in truth to be denied free will because he cannot sin?" Augustine assumes that everyone will want to call God free. One may ask the same question also about the righteous angels. But if God and the angels have free will, free will must be redefined so as to consist with a denial that two incompatible actions are equally possible. Free will must be made consistent with inevitability and therefore will no longer bear its common meaning.

Later writers also have made a point of the fixed and determined felicity of the future state, and it might be worth a parenthetical paragraph to pause for a reference to the Puritan John Gill. In *The Cause of God and Truth* (III, V, xiii) he writes,

> God is a most free agent, and liberty in him is in its utmost perfection, and yet does not lie in an indifference to good and evil; he has no freedom to that which is evil...his will is determined only to that which is good; he can do no other...and what he does, he does freely and yet necessarily.... The human nature of Christ, or the man Christ Jesus, who, as he was born without sin and lived without it all his days on Earth, so was impeccable, could not sin. He lay under some kind of necessity...to fulfill all righteousness; and yet he did it most freely and voluntarily: which proves that the liberty of man's will...is consistent with some kind of necessity.... The good angels, holy and elect, who are confirmed in the state in which they are...cannot sin or fall from that happy state, yet perform their whole obedience to God, do his will and work cheerfully and willingly.... In the state of glorification the saints will be impeccable, cannot sin, can only do that which is good, and yet what they do, or will do, is and will be done with the utmost freedom and liberty of their wills; whence it follows that the liberty of man's will...is consistent both with some kind of necessity and a determination to one.

In this age it is impossible for anyone not to sin. Sin is inevitable. Therefore the ability to do good or evil is not one.

This effectively disposes of Augustine's early contention that one must be able to sin in order to do anything good; it also leaves free will in a dubious condition.

In this material from Augustine and John Gill two important points emerge. The first is that the Bible does not teach the equal possibility of two incompatible choices. Even if some perverse misinterpreter should still contend that the ability to do good or evil is one, the meaning of the denial is plain and unambiguous. The second point that emerges from the preceding discussion is, however, a matter of ambiguity. Free will has been defined as the equal ability, under given circumstances, to choose either of two courses of action. No antecedent power determines the choice. Whatever motives or inclinations a man may have, or whatever inducements may be laid before him that might seem to turn him in a certain direction, he may at a moment disregard them all and do the opposite. This definition or description, however, is what the present writer believes to be the common notion of free will. It is not the definition found in Augustine or John Gill. Indeed these two writers do not give a formal definition of free will. Strange though it may seem to a logician, many writers do not define their terms with great care; and the reader is unfortunately left to guess at the meaning. An Arminian reading *The Cause of God and Truth* might very well wonder what its author could possibly mean by *liberty* and *freedom*. Nor would his perplexity be entirely unjustified. The Puritan speaks of a will that is both free and determined; he refers to actions that are done freely, yet necessarily; and he concludes that the liberty of a man's will is consistent with at least some kind of necessity and determination. But the Arminian reader feels himself almost necessitated to judge that this makes no sense. Are not necessity and freedom incompatible? Is it remotely possible that both could be attributed to the same action, choice, or will?

The explanation, of course, lies in the fact that the Arminian has a different notion of freedom from that of John Gill. And perhaps he is unaware that in the history of philosophy, freedom of choice has been defined in several different ways. One should never suppose that a phrase or a term means the same thing in every book in which it occurs. Each author chooses the meaning he desires, and each reader ought to try to determine what that meaning is. To be sure, the author ought not to try to make this task difficult, and Gill and others of his day should have said more clearly what they meant. Strict definitions and strict adherence to them are essential to intelligible discussion. If one contender has one idea in mind – or perhaps no clear idea at all, while the other party to the debate entertains a different notion, or is equally vague – the result of the conversation is bound to be complete confusion. This is the elementary lesson that Socrates taught in the fifth century before Christ, but many people have not learned it yet.

In accord with common opinion, the phrase *free will* shall here henceforth be used to indicate the theory that a man faced with incompatible courses of action is as able to choose any one as well as any other.

The Bible does not teach the equal possibility of two incompatible choices.

Strict definitions and strict adherence to them are essential to intelligible discussion.

It may be necessary in quoting previous authors to use the phrase in another sense, if they so used it; but the argument of this chapter will restrict the phrase *free will* to the above definition. This is done in the belief that no Arminian will object. He can make no accusation that his case is prejudged by a surreptitious introduction of a Calvinistic element into the chief term. *Free will* is defined with all the freedom that any Arminian could desire.

It might seem that here is the proper place to ask the question, Does man have a free will? Is it true that his choices are not determined by motives, by inducements, or by his settled character? Can a person resist God's grace and power and make an uncaused decision? However, these questions will not be answered here. They will be discussed later. The next step in the argument is a slightly different one. Let us assume that man's will is free; let us assume that these questions have been answered in the affirmative; it would still remain to be shown that free will solves the problem of evil. This then is the immediate inquiry. Is the theory of free will, even if true, a satisfactory explanation of evil in a world created by God? Reasons, compelling reasons, will now be given for a negative answer. Even if men were as able to choose good as evil, even if a sinner could choose Christ as easily as he could reject him, it would be totally irrelevant to the fundamental problem. Free will was put forward to relieve God of responsibility for sin. But this it does not do.

Suppose there were a lifeguard stationed on a dangerous beach. In the breakers a boy is being sucked out to sea by the strong undertow. He cannot swim. He will drown without powerful aid. It will have to be powerful, for as drowning sinners do, he will struggle against his rescuer. But the lifeguard simply sits on his high chair and watches him drown. Perhaps he may shout a few words of advice and tell him to exercise his free will. After all, it was of his own free will that the boy went into the surf. The guard did not push him in nor interfere with him in any way. The guard merely permitted him to go in and permitted him to drown. Would an Arminian now conclude that the lifeguard thus escapes culpability?

This illustration, with its finite limitations, is damaging enough as it is. It shows that permission of evil as contrasted with positive causality does not relieve a lifeguard from responsibility. Similarly, if God merely permits men to be engulfed in sin of their own free wills, the original objections of Voltaire and Professor Patterson are not thereby met. This is what the Arminian fails to notice. And yet the illustration does not do full justice to the actual situation. For unlike the boy who exists in relative independence of the lifeguard, in actuality God made the boy and the ocean, too. Now, if the guard – who is not a creator at all – is responsible for permitting the boy to drown, even if the boy is supposed to have entered the surf of his own free will, does not God – who made them – appear in a worse light? Surely an omnipotent God could have either made the boy a better swimmer, or made the ocean less rough, or at least have saved him from drowning.

Free will was put forward to relieve God of responsibility for sin. But this it does not do.

Not only are free will and permission irrelevant to the problem of evil, but, further, the idea of permission has no intelligible meaning. It is quite within the range of possibility for a lifeguard to permit a man to drown. This permission, however, depends on the fact that the ocean's undertow is beyond the guard's control. If the guard had some giant suction device which he operated so as to engulf the boy, one would call it murder, not permission. The idea of permission is possible only where there is an independent force, either the boy's force or the ocean's force. But this is not the situation in the case of God and the universe. Nothing in the universe can be independent of the omnipotent Creator, for in him we live and move and have our being. Therefore the idea of permission makes no sense when applied to God.

Such subterfuges must in all honesty be renounced. Consider two quotations from Calvin *(Institutes*, III, xxiii, 8; and II, iv, 3):

> Here they recur to the distinction between will and permission, and insist that God permits the destruction of the impious, but does not will it. But what reason shall we assign for his permitting it, but because it is his will? It is not probable, however, that man procured his own destruction by the mere permission, without any appointment, of God; as though God had not determined what he would choose to be the condition of the principal of his creatures. I shall not hesitate therefore to confess plainly with Augustine, "that the will of God is the necessity of things, and that what he has willed will necessarily come to pass."

> God is very frequently said to blind and harden the reprobate, and to turn, incline, and influence their hearts, as I have elsewhere more fully stated. But it affords no explication of the nature of this influence to resort to prescience or permission.... For the execution of his judgments, he, by means of Satan, the minister of his wrath, directs their counsels to what he pleases and excites their wills and strengthens their efforts. Thus when Moses relates that Sihon the king would not grant a free passage to the people, because God had "hardened his spirit and made his heart obstinate," he immediately subjoins the end of God's design: "That he might deliver him into thy hand." Since God willed his destruction, the obduration of his heart therefore was the divine preparation for his ruin.

Thus the futility of free will is established. Some other theory must be sought. And in the production of that theory it will become evident that free will is not only futile but false. Certainly, if the Bible is the Word of God, free will is false; for the Bible consistently denies free will. Therefore the attempt will now be made to explain evil on the basis of historic Protestantism.

Reformation Theology

So far this chapter has stated the paradox or antithesis between an omnipotent good God and the existence of evil. If free will cannot resolve the difficulty, one must turn to the opposite theory of determinism. At first, determinism, instead of alleviating the situation, seems to accentuate the problem of evil by maintaining the inevitability of every event; and not only the inevitability, but also the further and more embarrassing point that it is God himself who determines or decrees every action.

Some Calvinists prefer to avoid the word *determinism*. For some reason it seems to them to carry unpleasant connotations. However, the Bible speaks not only of predestination, usually with reference to eternal life, but it also speaks of the foreordination or predetermination of evil acts. Therefore, deliberate avoidance of the word *determinism* would seem to be less than forthright. This will be discussed still further later on. At the moment, however, there is a preliminary question. Do the opposing views, free will and determinism, form a complete disjunction?

The former holds that no human choice is determined; the latter that all are. Is there not a third possibility? Could it not be that some events or choices are determined and some are not? Such a third possibility, however, could contribute nothing to this discussion. Aside from the peculiarity of assigning a semi-sovereignty to God and to man a semi-free will, the crux of the conflict lies in choices that cannot be split in half. Could Judas have chosen not to betray Christ? If he could have chosen not to betray Christ, his moral responsibility is established, says the Arminian; but, says the Calvinist, prophecy in such a case could have proved false. Or, again, could Pilate have decided to release Jesus? Are we prepared to say that God could not make sure of the necessary events in his plan of redemption? Besides, the Bible explicitly says, "Herod and Pontius Pilate, with the Gentiles and the people of Israel, were gathered together to do whatever your hand and your purpose determined before to be done."[2] Here in these individual choices moral responsibility is pitted against the success of God's eternal plan of redemption. There is therefore no use in supposing some choices free and others determined. The Scriptures say that this one choice was determined ahead of time, and the whole theological and philosophical issue is found complete in this one choice.

It seems unnecessary to draw the contrast in any sharper terms. All the elements are before us: free will, determinism, moral responsibility, prophecy, and divine sovereignty versus a finite god. What is now necessary consists of three points which will provide the outline for the remainder of the chapter. First, some extensive explanation and argument in defense of Calvinism must be given; second, a definitive and official statement of the position should be provided; and third, a few historical assertions are demanded by the widespread ignorance of the twentieth century. These three points will be taken up in reverse order.

The low educational level of the present day, even among college people, was brought home to the present writer when he was asked to give an account of Calvinism to a group of students in a so-called Christian college. The talk was nothing more than the simplest and most elementary exposition of the famous five points. But at the end it

> *"Herod and Pontius Pilate, with the Gentiles and the people of Israel, were gathered together to do whatever your hand and your purpose determined before to be done."*

2. *Acts* 4:27-28.

became clear, with respect to the middle three – *i.e.*, unconditional election, limited atonement, and irresistible grace – not only that the students had never heard of such doctrines before, but that they were shocked that any professing Christian could possibly believe them. For two or three hundred years after the Reformation there was hardly a place or a section of the people in any of the Protestant nations that did not have a rudimentary knowledge of Calvinism. They may not all have believed the doctrines, but at least they had heard them preached. In the twentieth century, however, Christian knowledge has sunk to a very low level. Calvinism, of course, is not totally extinguished, but many people who think of themselves as educated Christians have never heard of it.

Today, therefore, we must insist that irresistible grace and divine determination were solid articles of the Reformation faith. Nor was it the Reformers who first discovered them.

Augustus M. Toplady, the author of that most beloved of all hymns, *Rock of Ages*, also wrote a good-sized volume on the *Historic Proof of the Doctrinal Calvinism of the Church of England*. A few pages later, he will be mentioned again more definitely with the main point of his book as stated in its title. But here attention is called to his long introductory section in which he shows that Calvinism was not unknown either in the Patristic period or in the Middle Ages.

Toplady believed that the epistle of *Barnabas* was actually written by Barnabas. If he is mistaken in this belief, the epistle is a still more noteworthy testimony to the doctrinal character of the subapostolic age. The following quotation seems to reflect the idea of irresistible grace and would therefore be inconsistent with free will: "When Christ chose his own Apostles who were to preach his gospel, he chose them when they were wickeder than all wickedness itself...." According to the same author, Christ's death was necessary because it was prophesied. And there is a fairly clear statement of limited atonement: "Let us rest assured, that the Son of God could not have suffered but for us." To the same effect he imagines Christ answering a question with the words, "I am to offer up my flesh as a sacrifice for the sins of the new people." A certain Menardus, commenting on this passage, complains that Barnabas was here mistaken because Christ did not die for a new people but for the whole world. The comment only emphasizes what Barnabas actually meant. A further negative note on free will is found in the words, "We...speak as the Lord wills us to speak. For that end he both circumcized our ears and our hearts that we might understand these things."³

Clement of Rome makes some very definite statements.

> It being the will of God that all his beloved ones should be made partakers of repentance, he has established them firmly by his own Almighty purpose.
>
> By the word of his Majesty he has established all things....Who shall say unto him, What have you done? Or who shall resist the might of his power? He has done all things at what season he pleased, and in what

Today, therefore, we must insist that irresistible grace and divine determination were solid articles of the Reformation faith.

Christ's death was necessary because it was prophesied.

3. *The Works of Augustus Toplady.* 1794, 82-83.

manner he pleased; and not one of the things which have been decreed by him shall pass away. All things are open to his view, nor has anything absconded from his will and pleasure.⁴

Ignatius begins his *Epistle to the Ephesians*, "Ignatius...predestinated ever, before time, unto the glory which is perpetual and unchangeable, united and chosen...by the will of the Father." He introduces his *Epistle to the Romans* with the words, "Enlightened by the will of him who has willed all things." And in opposition to free will he says, "A Christian is not the workmanship of suasion, but of greatness [power]."⁵

Perhaps it is better known, at least by those who have read some medieval history, that the martyr Gottschalk was a strong Calvinist. Speaking of the reprobate Jews he says, "Our Lord perceived that they were predestinated to everlasting destruction, and were not purchased with the price of his blood."⁶ After twenty-one years of imprisonment and torture at the hands of Bishop Hincmar for his belief in double predestination, he died A.D. 870.

Less well known is a contemporary of Gottschalk, Remigus, archbishop of Lyons. He wrote,

> Nor is it possible for any one elect person to perish, or that any of the reprobate should be saved, because of their hardness and impenitency of heart.... Almighty God did, from the beginning, prior to the formation of the world, and before he had made any thing, predestinate...some certain persons to glory, of his own gratuitous favor.... Other certain persons he has predestinated to perdition...and of these, none can be saved.⁷

The Waldensians were a group whose origin Toplady puts early in the Middle Ages. He quotes from their *Confession of 1508*: "It is manifest that such only as are elected to glory become partakers of true faith."

A hundred years before the Reformation, Jan Hus said, "Predestination does make a man a member of the universal Church.... God wills that the predestinate shall have perpetual blessedness, and the reprobate to have eternal fire. The predestinate cannot fall from grace."⁸ Obviously there is no free will here.

If Hus was burnt for the Gospel, John of Wesalia was tortured because he held that "God has, from everlasting, written a book, wherein he has inscribed all his elect; and whosoever is not already written there will never be written there at all. Moreover, he that is written therein will never be blotted out of it."⁹

After these continental Calvinists, Toplady turns to pre-Reformation Englishmen. Venerable Bede said, "When Pelagius asserts that we are at liberty to do one thing always [*i.e.*, to do good], seeing we are always able to do both one and the other [*i.e.*, we have free will], he herein contradicts the prophet, who, humbly addressing himself to God, says, 'I know, O Lord, that a man's way is not his own; it is not in man that walks to direct his own steps.'"¹⁰

Thomas Bradwardine, the teacher of John Wycliffe, wrote,

"God has, from everlasting, written a book, wherein he has inscribed all his elect; and whosoever is not already written there will never be written there at all. Moreover, he that is written therein will never be blotted out of it."

— John of Wesalia

---

4. Toplady, 84.
5. Toplady, 87-88.
6. Toplady, 93.
7. Toplady, 94.
8. Toplady, 97.
9. Toplady, 98.
10. Toplady, 100.

What multitudes, O Lord, at this day, join hands with Pelagius in contending for free will and in fighting against thy absolutely free grace.... Some more haughty than Lucifer,...dread not to affirm, that, even in a common action, their own will walks first, as an independent mistress, and that thy will follows after, like an obsequious handmaid.... [T]he will of God is universally efficacious and invincible, and necessitates as a cause. It cannot be impeded, much less can it be defeated and made void, by any means whatever.[11]

His pupil, John Wycliffe (A.D. 1320? – 1384), similarly declared, "In what way soever God may declare his will by his after-discoveries of it in time: still, his determination, concerning the event, took place before the world was made; *ergo*, the event will surely follow. The necessity, therefore, of the antecedent, holds no less irrefragably for the necessity of the consequent."

Dr. Peter Heylin, an Arminian historian, admits that William Tyndal "has a flying-out against free will" and taught that from predestination "it springeth altogether whether we shall believe or not believe, be loosed from sin or not be loosed; by which predestination our justifying and salvation are clear taken out of our hands and put into the hands of God only." The Arminian with his free will does not want his salvation put into the hands of God only.

Patrick Hamilton's sentence of death read: "We, James, by the mercy of God, archbishop of St. Andrews, primate of Scotland, have found Master Patrick Hamilton many ways inflamed with heresy...that man hath no free will."[12]

The struggles of these loyal exponents of the Gospel of free grace culminated in the Protestant Reformation. At the Council of Trent, the Roman Church officially repudiated the doctrines that put salvation into the hands of God only. Rome chose free will and human merit. Luther and Calvin continued the apostolic teaching. In our present century of ignorance, one must insist that Luther as well as Calvin rejected the Pelagian-Romish-Arminian view of man. It was Erasmus, the man who drew back from the Reformation and made his peace with Rome, who defended free will. The book that Luther wrote in reply to him is titled *The Bondage of the Will*. In its Conclusion there is this sentence: "For if we believe it to be true that God foreknows and foreordains all things, that he can neither be deceived nor hindered in his prescience and predestination, and that nothing can take place but according to his will...then there can be no free will in man, in angel, or in any creature."

While the later Lutherans – under Phillip Melanchthon's compromising spirit, which went so far as to seek reunion with Rome – abandoned many of Luther's doctrines, it must be remembered that these matters were not in dispute among Luther, Zwingli, and Calvin, nor among Ridley, Cranmer, Latimer, Bucer, Zanchius, and Knox. The same is true of the victims of Bloody Mary. Richard Woodman, who was burned at the stake with nine other martyrs at Lewes in Sussex, answered his examiners: "If we have free will, then our salvation cometh

---

"For if we believe it to be true that God foreknows and foreordains all things, that he can neither be deceived nor hindered in his prescience and predestination, and that nothing can take place but according to his will...then there can be no free will in man, in angel, or in any creature."
– Martin Luther

11. Toplady, 106-108.
12. Of these quotations by Toplady I have verified those I could easily find. Others are relatively inaccessible. Since Toplady often gives the Latin text, one may hope that he has been accurate. If in some place he has made a mistake, it is still proved that the five points did not originate with Calvin, much less with the Synod of Dordt.

of ourselves: which is a great blasphemy against God and his Word." Richard Gibson, examined by the Bishop of London, was called upon to profess that "a man hath by God's grace a free choice and will in his doing." Gibson denied the proposition and was burned to death with two others in Smithfield. Thirty-four persons were persecuted and expelled from the towns of Winston and Mendelsham, because "they denied man's free will and held that the Pope's church did err." If more evidence is desired for the Calvinism of the Reformation, there is an abundance of it in the history books and in the original writings of these faithful men.

In the non-Lutheran world the Reformation faith was first adulterated by Arminius, who, influenced by Melanchthonian Lutheranism, rejected the Reformed view of free grace and retreated to a more Romish or semi-Pelagian position. The Synod of Dordt in 1618 condemned Arminius as a corrupter of the faith, though it did not rise to the explicit heights of the Westminster Assembly thirty years later. It is the latter's *Confession* that is the highwater mark of Protestantism. No other creed is so detailed and so true to the Scriptures. Therefore the present day reader is requested to give exact attention to a quotation from the *Westminster Confession*. Though some circumscribed souls may be astonished, this is what Christianity is.

> *"God from all eternity did, by the most wise and holy counsel of his own will, freely and unchangeably ordain whatsoever comes to pass; yet so, as thereby neither is God the author of sin, nor is violence offered to the will of the creatures, nor is the liberty or contingency of second causes taken away, but rather established.... By the decree of God, for the manifestation of his glory, some men and angels are predestinated unto everlasting life, and others foreordained to everlasting death."*
> *— Westminster Confession of Faith*

CHAPTER THREE
OF GOD'S ETERNAL DECREE

I. God from all eternity did, by the most wise and holy counsel of his own will, freely and unchangeably ordain whatsoever comes to pass; yet so, as thereby neither is God the author of sin, nor is violence offered to the will of the creatures, nor is the liberty or contingency of second causes taken away, but rather established.

II. Although God knows whatsoever may or can come to pass upon all supposed conditions, yet has he not decreed anything because he foresaw it as future, or as that which would come to pass upon such conditions.

III. By the decree of God, for the manifestation of his glory, some men and angels are predestinated unto everlasting life, and others foreordained to everlasting death.

IV. These angels and men, thus predestinated and foreordained, are particularly and unchangeably designed; and their number is so certain and definite, that it cannot be either increased or diminished.

V. Those of mankind that are predestinated unto life, God, before the foundation of the world was laid, according to his eternal and immutable purpose and the secret counsel and good pleasure of his will, has chosen in Christ unto everlasting glory, out of his mere free grace and love, without any foresight of faith, or good works, or perseverance in either of them, or any other thing in the creature, as conditions, or causes moving him thereunto; and all to the praise of his glorious grace.

VI. As God has appointed the elect unto glory, so has he, by the eternal and most free purpose of his will, foreordained all the means thereunto. Wherefore, they who are elected, being fallen in Adam, are redeemed by Christ, are effectually called unto faith in Christ by his

Spirit working in due season, are justified, adopted, sanctified, and kept by his power, through faith, unto salvation. Neither are any other redeemed by Christ, effectually called, justified, adopted, sanctified, and saved, but the elect only.

VII. The rest of mankind God was pleased, according to the unsearchable counsel of his own will, whereby he extends or withholds mercy as he pleases, for the glory of his sovereign power over his creatures, to pass by; and to ordain them to dishonor and wrath for their sin, to the praise of his glorious justice.

VIII. The doctrine of this high mystery of predestination is to be handled with special prudence and care, that men, attending the will of God revealed in his word, and yielding obedience thereunto, may, from the certainty of their effectual vocation, be assured of their eternal election. So shall this doctrine afford matter of praise, reverence, and admiration of God, and of humility, diligence, and abundant consolation to all that sincerely obey the Gospel.

This official statement of the original Protestant position, of the original apostolic faith, concludes this historical section. The next step is to give some of the arguments that support Calvinism and to apply these considerations to the problem of evil.

Gill's Exegesis

Although the *Westminster Confession* is the most detailed of all creeds, it is still not a philosophic treatise. It is not a theodicy. It does not answer objections. It is only a summary of the Biblical position. In this respect, and so far as exegesis goes, Arminianism cannot compete. Not to suppose that the Westminster divines were the only men who saw these teachings in the Bible, one may refer again to John Gill's *The Cause of God and Truth*. The first two parts of that work examine with great care more than a hundred passages which Arminians had used in opposition to Calvinism. Gill's exegesis is devastating.

Since the approximately 150 pages, double columns, of fairly dense type, cannot be reproduced here, one example alone will be chosen. It is a verse which, according to Gill, was frequently quoted by the Arminians of his day, but quoted incorrectly, and which has been several times used against the present writer: "O Jerusalem, Jerusalem, you that kill the prophets, and stone them that are sent to you, how often would I have gathered your children together, even as a hen gathers her chickens under her wings, and you would not!" (*Matthew* 23:37).

Concerning this verse John Gill observes,

> Nothing is more common in the mouths and writings of the Arminians than this Scripture, which they are ready to produce on every occasion against the doctrines of election and reprobation, particular redemption, and the irresistible power of God in conversion; and in favor of sufficient grace and of free will and power in man; though to very little purpose, as will appear when the following things are observed.

"Neither are any other redeemed by Christ, effectually called, justified, adopted, sanctified, and saved, but the elect only."

1. That by *Jerusalem* we are not to understand the city, nor all the inhabitants, but the rulers and governors of it, both civil and ecclesiastical, especially the great Sanhedrin, which was held in it, to whom best belong the descriptive characters of killing the prophets and stoning such as were sent to them by God, and who are manifestly distinguished from their children; it being usual to call such who were the heads of the people, either in a civil or ecclesiastical sense, *fathers*, Acts 7:2, and 22: 1, and such who were subjects and disciples, *children*, 19:44, Matthew 12:27, Isaiah 8:16, 18. Besides, our Lord's discourse, throughout the whole context, is directed to the Scribes and Pharisees, the ecclesiastical guides of the people, and to whom the civil governors paid a special regard. Hence it is manifest, that they are not the same persons whom Christ would have gathered, who would not. It is not said, *How often would I have gathered you, and ye would not*, as Dr. Whitby more than once inadvertently cites the text; nor, *he would have gathered Jerusalem and she would not*, as the same author transcribes it in another place; nor, *he would have gathered them, thy children, and they would not*, in which form it is also sometimes expressed by him; but *I would have gathered thy children, and ye would not*, which observation alone is sufficient to destroy the argument founded on this passage in favor of free will....

5. That in order to set aside and overthrow the doctrines of election, reprobation, and particular redemption, it should be proved that Christ, as God, would have gathered, not Jerusalem and the inhabitants thereof only, but all mankind, even such as are not eventually saved, and that in a spiritual saving way and manner to himself, of which there is not the least intimation in this text; and in order to establish the resistibility of God's grace, by the perverse will of man, so as to become of no effect, it should be proved that Christ would have savingly converted these persons, and they would not be converted; and that he bestowed the same grace upon them he does bestow on others who are converted; whereas the sum of this passage lies in these few words, that Christ, as man, out of a compassionate regard for the people of the Jews, to whom he was sent, would have gathered them together under his ministry, and have instructed them in the knowledge of himself as Messiah; which, if they had only notionally received, would have secured them as chickens under the hen from impending judgments which afterwards fell on them; but their governors, and not they, would not, that is, would not suffer them to be collected together in such a manner, and hindered all they could, their giving any credit to him as the Messiah; though had it been said *and they would not*, it would only have been a most sad instance of the perverseness of the will of man, which often opposes his temporal as well as his spiritual good.

On the ground of exegesis, therefore, Calvinism has nothing to fear; but further development of the doctrine, the integration of one phase with another, the application to the problem of evil, and the replies to objections are left in the hands of theologians and philosophers of religion rather than with exegetes or creedal assemblies. And it may be granted that John Gill's theological elucidations, by reason of incomplete expression, absence of definition, failure to foresee later scientific theories, and even quirks of his own reasoning, are not always so successful as his exegesis of Scripture.

> *"In order to set aside and overthrow the doctrines of election, reprobation, and particular redemption, it should be proved that Christ, as God, would have gathered, not Jerusalem and the inhabitants thereof only, but all mankind...."*
> –John Gill

For example, when Dr. Whitby – John Gill's opponent – charges the Calvinists with implying that God intends to damn the wicked (and certain other matters that Dr. Whitby finds offensive), it is not sufficient to reply with Gill that the Calvinists do not make these assertions. For, first, possibly some of them do; and, second, even if no Calvinist made these assertions, Dr. Whitby's horrors might be valid, though hitherto unrecognized, implications from Calvinistic principles. A theologian is therefore under obligation to answer the charge of inconsistency in such a case, even though Dr. Whitby is himself many times more inconsistent. We shall pass then from exegesis to theological discussion.

Omniscience

Not only does free will fail to relieve God of culpability, and permission fail to coexist with omnipotence, but the Arminian position can find no logical position for omniscience either. A Romanist-Arminian illustration is that of an observer on a high cliff. On the road below, to the observer's left, a car is being driven west. To the observer's right a car is coming south. He can see and know that there will be a collision at the intersection immediately beneath him. But his foreknowledge, so the argument runs, does not cause the accident. Similarly, God is supposed to know the future without causing it.

The similarity, however, is deceptive on several points. A human observer cannot really know that a collision will occur. Though it is unlikely, it is possible for both cars to have blowouts before reaching the intersection and swerve apart. It is also possible that the observer has misjudged the speeds, in which case one car could slow down and the other accelerate, so that they would not collide. The human observer, therefore, does not have infallible foreknowledge.

No such mistakes can be assumed for God. The human observer may make a probable guess that the accident will occur, and this guess does not make the accident unavoidable; but if God knows, there is no possibility of avoiding the accident. A hundred years before the drivers were born, there was no possibility of avoiding the accident. There was no possibility that either one of them could have chosen to stay home that day, to have driven a different route, to have driven a different time, to have driven a different speed. They could not have chosen otherwise than as they did. This means either that they had no free will or that God did not know.

Suppose it be granted, just for the moment, that divine foreknowledge, like human guesses, does not cause the foreknown event. Even so, if there is foreknowledge, in contrast with fallible guesses, free will is impossible. If man has free will, and things can be different, God cannot be omniscient. Some Arminians have admitted this and have denied omniscience, but this puts them obviously at odds with Biblical Christianity. There is also another difficulty. If the Arminian or Romanist wishes to retain divine omniscience and at the same time assert that foreknowledge has no causal efficacy, he is put to it to ex-

Not only does free will fail to relieve God of culpability, and permission fail to coexist with omnipotence, but the Arminian position can find no logical position for omniscience either.

plain how the collision was made certain a hundred years, an eternity, before the drivers were born. If God did not arrange the universe this way, who did?

If God did not arrange it this way, then there must be an independent factor in the universe. And if there is such, one consequence and perhaps two follow. First, the doctrine of creation must be abandoned. A creation *ex nihilo* would be completely in God's control. Independent forces cannot be created forces, and created forces cannot be independent. Then, second, if the universe is not God's creation, his knowledge of it – past and future – cannot depend on what he intends to do, but on his observation of how it works. In such a case, how could we be sure that God's observations are accurate? How could we be sure that these independent forces will not later show an unsuspected twist that will falsify God's predictions? And, finally, on this view God's knowledge would be empirical, rather than an integral part of his essence, and thus he would be a dependent knower. These objections are insurmountable. We can consistently believe in creation, omnipotence, omniscience, and the divine decree. But we cannot retain sanity and combine any one of these with free will.[13]

Responsibility and Free Will

Free will, however, was introduced into the picture for very definite reasons. Since it is so at variance with basic Christian doctrines, there must have been exceptionally strong inducements for taking refuge in it. These are the necessity of maintaining human responsibility for sin and of preserving the righteousness of God. The Arminian may be willing to admit that his view faces difficulties; but, he asks, can the Calvinist offer a better escape? It is all well and good to show the conflict between omnipotent creation and free will, but what about the conflict between determinism and morality? Is it not better to take a strong stand for morality and responsibility, even if we degrade God to a finite level, than to defend omnipotence so as to undermine human morality and divine holiness? In other words, since God cannot be both omnipotent and good, is it not better to admit a finite god?

Perhaps one quotation may be allowed to document the dependence of free will on the motive of responsibility, but before that is done, let it be noted that there is no other motive. Could it be shown that man's responsibility does not presuppose free will, theology would be freed from all this confusion. No longer would one be required to hold half-heartedly to one set of self-contradictory doctrines rather than to a second set of equally contradictory doctrines. Nor would one be compelled to disguise the obvious contradictions by the false piety of calling them mysteries. The remainder of the argument will attempt to show that neither human responsibility nor divine holiness requires free will. But first the quotation just alluded to:

> Throughout the whole history of philosophy and theology people have wrangled over the question of free will. In general, the idealistic

13. For further argument, see Jonathan Edwards, *Miscellaneous Observations*, Part II, chapter 3; 1811 edition, Volume VIII, 384.

philosophies have asserted that the human spirit must be in some sense free, while materialistic philosophies have denied this freedom. Theology has clung tenaciously to the belief that man is a "free moral agent" while at the same time often asserting a doctrine of predestination which, taken at its face value, would rigidly circumscribe man's acts. The problem, though complex, is too fundamental to be dodged.

We have seen that the possibility of moral or immoral action depends on the power of choice. If all one's acts are set and predetermined (either by the structure of the material world or by the will of God) in such fashion that it is impossible to act other than one does, quite obviously freedom disappears. With the power of voluntary choice goes moral responsibility. One cannot consciously choose to be good, nor choose to seek after God, unless he has the power to choose not to do so. No moral quality attaches to my failure to steal the million dollars that is outside my reach, but stealing becomes a moral question with me when I have to decide whether to tell the store clerk he has given me too much change. Likewise if I am "foreordained" to be saved or damned there is not much use of my doing anything about my fate. If I have no freedom, I am not responsible for my acts.

Theological determinism, or predestination, is a cardinal doctrine of Mohammedanism. Islam means "submission" (to the will of Allah) and a Moslem is "one who submits" to the fatalistic decrees of an arbitrary deity. Christian theology in its earlier forms regarded God as equally peremptory (though more ethical) in his decrees. Through the influence of illustrious Christian theologians, notably Paul, Augustine, and Calvin, the doctrine of predestination has profoundly influenced Christian thinking. While God's omnipotence has thus been emphasized, God's freedom has been exalted at the expense of man's, and the most inhuman acts have been glossed over as arising from the will of God. But happily the doctrine of predestination is disappearing, at least in its application to evils that are obviously preventable.

Some still hold that when the typhoid victim dies from lack of proper sanitation, it happened because it was "to be." There is a good deal of illogical comfort in such a view. But not many, even of the most rigorous of Calvinists, would now say that if a man gets drunk and shoots his family, it is the will of God that he should do so.[14]

The Will of God

This quotation shows clearly the moral motivation behind the theory of free will; but at the same time it shows so much muddleheadedness, misstatement of facts, and fallacious innuendo that before the argument proceeds, one preliminary should be put out of the way. I wish very frankly and pointedly to assert that if a man gets drunk and shoots his family, it was the will of God that he should do so. The Scriptures leave no room for doubt, as was made plain before, that it was God's will for Herod, Pilate, and the Jews to crucify Christ. In *Ephesians* 1:11 Paul tells us that God works all things, not some things only, after the counsel of his own will. This is essential to the doctrine of creation. Before the world was made, God knew everything that was to happen; with this knowledge he willed that these things should come to pass.

I wish very frankly and pointedly to assert that if a man gets drunk and shoots his family, it was the will of God that he should do so.

14. Georgia Harkness, *Conflict in Religious Thought*, 233-234.

Only if God had been willing could this world, or any world, in all its details, have been brought into existence.

The opponents may at this point claim that Calvinism introduces a self-contradiction into the will of God. Is not murder contrary to the will of God? How then can God will it?

Very easily. The term *will* is ambiguous. The Ten Commandments are God's preceptive will. They command men to do this and to refrain from that. They state what *ought* to be done; but they neither state nor cause what is done. God's decretive will, however, as contrasted with his precepts, causes every event. It would be conducive to clarity if the term *will* were not applied to the precepts. Call the requirements of morality *commands, precepts,* or *laws*; and reserve the term *will* for the divine decree. These are two different things, and what looks like an opposition between them is not a self-contradiction. The Jews ought not to have demanded Christ's crucifixion. It was contrary to the moral law. But God had decreed Christ's death from the foundation of the world. It may seem strange at first that God would decree an immoral act, but the Bible shows that he did. This point will be discussed more fully later on; but though it may now seem strange, it should be clear at least that a clear definition of terms by which two different things are not confused under one name removes the charge of self-contradiction.

When the term *will* is used loosely there is also a second distinction that must be made. One may speak of the secret will of God, and one may speak of the revealed will of God. Those who saw self-contradiction in the previous case would no doubt argue similarly on this point too. The Arminian would say that God's will cannot contradict itself, and that therefore his secret will cannot contradict his revealed will. Now, the Calvinist would say the same thing; but he has a clearer notion of what contradiction is, and what the Scriptures say. It was God's secret will that Abraham should not sacrifice his son Isaac; but it was his revealed will (for a time), his command, that he should do so. Superficially this seems like a contradiction. But it is not. The statement or command, "Abraham, sacrifice Isaac," does not contradict the statement, at that moment known only to God, "I have decreed that Abraham shall not sacrifice his son." If Arminians had a keener sense of logic they would not be Arminians!

If Arminians had a keener sense of logic they would not be Arminians!

Puppets

Confusion sometimes borders on ridicule. To come one step nearer to the question of human responsibility, another phrase from the opponents begs for analysis. Among many others, Professor Stuart C. Hackett charges that Calvinistic determinism reduces men to mere puppets.

Professor Hackett is engaged in resurrecting the theism of the cosmological argument. In this endeavor he opposes a theory called presuppositionalism on the ground that it is based on a previously adopted theological position. This of course is what the present book has done; these chapters have presuppositions and attention has been called to them; but Professor Hackett's apparent inference is that such a procedure should be avoided. Yet, strange to say, his final and clinching reason for rejecting presuppositionalism is, "Thus the presuppositionalist approach lands one in an extreme Calvinistic atmosphere. If one feels comfortable there, let him remain with this God who has created rational men as mere puppets of his sovereignty."[15]

Here there are two points. The minor point is that Professor Hackett in arguing against presuppositionalism adopts his own presuppositions. Of course, his presuppositions are Arminian, but even so he has not escaped presuppositionalism. The major point, however, is that Calvinism is supposed to reduce men to puppets.

Such an objection could arise only upon an ignorance of Puritan writings. Perhaps the objector has seen a chapter in the *Westminster Confession* "On Free Will"; or he may have read in the *Shorter Catechism* that our first parents were left to the freedom of their own wills; then, without reading the literature of that day, he assumes that official Calvinism is more moderate than the view defended here, and that a denial of free will is hyper-Calvinism. A creed, however, is not a detailed philosophic treatise, and its phrases must be understood in the sense in which the authors meant them. If this meaning is not clear from the creedal context itself, it must be sought in the literature.

Now, the *Westminster Confession* indeed speaks of the natural liberty of man's will. The first paragraph of Chapter IX is: "God has endued the will of man with that natural liberty that is neither forced, nor, by any absolute necessity of nature, determined to good or evil."

These phrases could seem to be accommodations to the theory of free will, but they can seem so only because the meaning of the phrase "absolute necessity of nature" has been mistaken. *The Reformation Principles*, a part of the standards of the Reformed Presbyterian Church, makes a clearer statement when it condemns as an error the view that man "is necessarily impelled to choose or act as an unconscious machine." Even the earlier seventeenth-century phrases must have seemed unambiguous when they were written, for they were chosen against the background of a century of discussion. They are certainly to be taken in a sense consistent with the *Confession's* chapter on the divine decree. Here again the *Reformation Principles* is quite clear, for the immediately following error denounced is "that he can will or act independently of the purpose or the providence of God." If the meaning of these phrases has been forgotten by some present-day writers, the remedy lies in reading the discussion of the seventeenth and eighteenth centuries.

First, some material again from John Gill will be put in evidence. Gill is chosen particularly because he was not a Presbyterian. It needs to be recalled that these ideas were not limited to the Presbyterians. For Gill's extended context, see *The Cause of God and Truth*, Part III.

The actions of glorified saints, he says, are done in obedience to the will of God; these acts proceed from the saints freely, though their wills

Professor Hackett in arguing against presuppositionalism adopts his own presuppositions.

Gill is chosen particularly because he was not a Presbyterian. It needs to be recalled that these ideas were not limited to the Presbyterians.

15. *The Resurrection of Theism*, 174

are immutably determined so that they can never do otherwise – sin is impossible in Heaven. By these phrases Gill shows that the term *freely* is consistent with immutable determinism.

That action, he says again, which is voluntarily committed against the law of God is blameworthy, though the will may be influenced and determined to it by the corruption of nature; because sin is no less sinful because man has so corrupted his way that he cannot do otherwise. Thus Gill connects responsibility with volition or will, but the will is not a free will because the man cannot do otherwise.

In opposing the materialistic philosophy of Thomas Hobbes, John Gill states that the question is whether all agents and events are predetermined extrinsically without their own concurrence in the determination. The dispute with Mr. Hobbes, he continues, is not about the power of the will to do this or that, but about the natural liberty of the will. This line of argument makes the natural liberty of the will to consist in its freedom from extrinsic or materialistic causes. Hobbes, if anyone does, makes man a puppet, because man's actions are completely determined by physico-chemical causes. This is, of course, one form of determinism, but it has never been Calvinistic determinism; and to charge against Calvinism what may no doubt be properly charged against Hobbes only shows ignorance of the Calvinistic position.

More at length John Gill says that the necessity we contend for, that the will of man lies under, is a necessity of immutability and infallibility with respect to the divine decrees – which have their necessary, unchangeable, and certain event: All which is consistent with the natural liberty of the will. We say that the will is free from a necessity of coaction and force and from a physical necessity of nature, such as that by which the Sun, Moon, and stars move in their course.

Although this has not been a continuous, verbatim quotation, the phraseology is Gill's; and as it is very instructive, it should be strictly noted. The natural liberty of the will consists in a freedom from physical necessity. Choice is not determined as the planetary motions are. Physical or mechanical determinism, expressible in differential equations, is applicable only to inanimate objects; but there is a psychological determinism that is not mechanical or mathematical. The Calvinist repudiates the former but accepts the latter. Hence he may without inconsistency deny free will and yet speak of a natural liberty.

Later on, when discussing Stoicism, Gill notes that Augustine did not care for the connotation of the term *Fate*, but that he had no objection to the thing itself. And Gill adds, we agree with the Stoics when they assert that all things that happen are determined by God from eternity. Some of the Stoics were very careful to preserve the natural liberty of the will, as we are; for example, Chrysippus taught that the will was free from the necessity of motion.

John Gill was a Baptist. In order further to avoid dependence on Presbyterian sources and to show that these are the doctrines of Protestantism, a few lines will be taken from the enthusiastic Anglican, our previous friend, Augustus Toplady – now as a theologian rather than as

Hobbes, if anyone does, makes man a puppet, because man's actions are completely determined by physico-chemical causes.

an historian. The first reference comes at the end of section eight of his history. To the sentence, "Calvinism disclaims all compulsion, properly so called," he appends a footnote in which he defines compulsion as taking place "when the beginning or continuing of any action is contrary to the preference of the mind.... In the supernatural agency of grace on the heart, compulsion is quite excluded, be that agency ever so effectual; since the more effectually it is supposed to operate, the more certainly it must engage 'the preference of the mind.'" The footnote continues on this theme for several more lines.

Space forbids the reproduction of a great amount of material, but one further reference may be taken from Toplady. In a work titled *The Scheme of Christian and Philosophical Necessity Asserted*, there are the following sentiments.

Let us, he says, by defining as we go, ascertain what free agency (in opposition to free will) is. All needless refinements apart, free agency, in plain English, is neither more nor less than voluntary agency. Now, necessity is to be defined as that by which whatever comes to pass cannot but come to pass, and can come to pass in no other way than it does. I acquiesce, says Toplady, in the old distinction – adopted by Luther and by most of, not to say all, the sound Reformed divines – between a necessity of compulsion and a necessity of infallible certainty. The necessity of compulsion is predicated of inanimate bodies and even of reasonable beings when they are forced to do or suffer anything contrary to their will and choice. The necessity of infallible certainty, on the other hand, renders the event inevitably future, without any compulsory force on the will of the agent. Thus Judas was a necessary though voluntary actor in that tremendous business.

It would be well to read the entire treatise, but enough has been indicated to enable us to come closer to our conclusion. In the theological literature, free agency – or natural liberty – means that the will is not determined by physical or physiological factors. But free agency is not free will. Free will means that there is no determining factor operating on the will, not even God. Free will means that either of two incompatible actions are equally possible. Free agency goes with the view that all choices are inevitable. The liberty that the *Westminster Confession* ascribes to the will is a liberty from compulsion, coaction, or force of inanimate objects; it is not a liberty from the power of God.

Perhaps the matter can be made clearer by stating in other words precisely what the question is. The question is, Is the will free? The question is not, Is there a will? Calvinism most assuredly holds that Judas acted voluntarily. He chose to betray Christ. He did so willingly. No question is raised as to whether or not he had a will. What the Calvinist asks is whether that will was free. Are there factors or powers that determine a person's choice, or is the choice causeless? Could Judas have chosen otherwise? Not, could he have done otherwise, had he chosen; but, could he have chosen in opposition to God's foreordination? *Acts 4:28* indicates that he could not. The Arminians frequently talk as if the will and free will were synonyms. Then when Calvinism

> "In the supernatural agency of grace on the heart, compulsion is quite excluded, be that agency ever so effectual; since the more effectually it is supposed to operate, the more certainly it must engage 'the preference of the mind.'"
> – *John Gill*

denies free will, they charge that men are reduced to puppets. Puppets, of course, are inanimate dolls mechanically controlled by strings. If the opponents had only read the Puritans, if they only had known what Calvinism is, they could have spared themselves the onus of making this blunder.

Choice and necessity are therefore not incompatible. Instead of prejudging the question by confusing choice with free choice, one should give an explicit definition of choice. The adjective could be justified only afterward, if at all. Choice then may be defined, at least sufficiently for the present purpose, as a mental act that consciously initiates and determines a further action. The ability to have chosen otherwise is an irrelevant matter and has no place in the definition. Such an ability could only be argued after the definition has been made. We cannot permit the Arminians to settle the whole matter simply by selecting a definition. A choice is still a deliberate volition even if it could not have been different.

Appeal to Ignorance

In fact, it is not possible to know that it could have been different, for we are unconscious of our limitations. The opponents frequently rest their case for free will on their own consciousness of freedom. It seems immediately and introspectively clear to them that their choices are uncaused. But such a view assumes that they would be conscious of causality, if there were any. To see that this is not the case, one may try to specify the conditions under which a man could know that he had a free will.

We observe in children and sometimes in adults atypical forms of conduct that we ascribe to fatigue (the child is fussy because he has missed his nap) or to nervous strain (the adult blows his top or takes to alcohol). The individuals in question are acting voluntarily and may well believe that their choices are uncaused. We know better. We know what the causes are, and we know that they do not recognize them. Although it is easy to see this in the case of other people, there is a tendency to overlook the fact that the same is true of ourselves. We usually assume that nothing is affecting our own will, just because we are not conscious of the causality. But how could we be sure that there is no cause? What conditions would have to be met before we could know that nothing is determining our choices? Not only would we have to eliminate the possibility of fatigue and nervous strain, but we would have to eliminate other factors that are neither so easily examined after we think of them nor so easily thought of in the first place. There are minute physiological conditions beyond our usual or possible range of attention. Some incipient disease may be affecting our minds. There are also external meteorological factors, for admittedly unpleasant weather is depressing. And can we be sure that a sun spot, whose existence we do not suspect, leaves us unaffected? Even though the will is not mechanically determined, these external conditions as well as our physiology seem to alter our conduct to some extent. More important than physiology and astronomy is psychology. May there not be some subconscious jealousy that motivates our reactions to other people? Why do we eat chocolate sundaes when we know that we should reduce? Are we free from the influence of parental training? The Scriptures say, "Train up a child in the way he should go, and when he is old he will not depart from it." Parental training and all education proceed on the assumption that the will is not free, but can be trained, motivated, and directed. Finally, beyond both physiology and psychology there is God. Can we be sure that he is not directing our choices? Do we know that we are free from his grace? The *Psalm* says, "Blessed is the man whom you choose and cause to approach you." Is it certain that God has not caused us to choose to approach him? Can we set a limit to God's power? Can we tell how far it extends and just where it ends? Are we outside his control?

The conclusion is evident, is it not? In order to know that our wills are determined by no cause, we should have to know every possible cause in the entire universe. Nothing could be allowed to escape our mind. To be conscious of free will therefore requires omniscience. Hence there is no consciousness of free will; what its exponents take as consciousness of free will is simply the unconsciousness of determination.

This disposes of those trivial examples in which we are told that the choice between cherry pie and apple pie is totally uncaused. Such cases do not do justice to the gravity of the subject. If, however, examples are requested, one might take Luther's choice: Here I stand, so help me God, I can do no other. With the greater consciousness of the issues involved comes a lesser assurance that an alternative is possible.

Responsibility and Determinism

Yet Luther was responsible for his choice, necessary though it was. Free will is not the basis of responsibility. In the first place, and at a more superficial level, the basis of responsibility is knowledge. The sinfulness of the Gentiles, as stated in the first chapter of *Romans*, could be charged to them because – although they did not like to retain God in their knowledge – they did not entirely succeed in their attempt to forget him; throughout their sinning they still knew the judgment of God that they which commit such things are worthy of death. This knowledge no doubt is an innate knowledge; it did not come from the Scriptures, but is the remains of the original image of God in which he created man. To the same effect is *Luke* 12:47, "And that servant who knew his master's will, and did not prepare himself or do according to his will, shall be beaten with many stripes. But he who did not know, yet committed things worthy of stripes, shall be beaten with few."

The explanation of responsibility, however, goes deeper than knowledge. Indeed, if we take responsibility in its fullest extent, and if we admit that we are made guilty in virtue of the first sin of our federal head, Adam, it follows that our responsibility is not ultimately based on our choice at all. *Romans* 5:17 reads, "by one man's offense death reigned through the one," and the passage goes on (verse 19) to say, "as by one man's disobedience many were made sinners, so also by one man's obedience will many be made righteous." In conformity with the Scriptures, the *Westminster Confession* declares, "They being the root of all mankind, the guilt of this sin was imputed; and the same death in sin, and corrupted nature, conveyed to all their posterity descending from them by ordinary generation" (VI, iii). Responsibility, therefore, must be so defined as to make room for imputation, as well as to account for our everyday voluntary actions.

It is strange that theological literature has made so little attempt to define *responsibility*. It is a lack found among determinists and indeterminists alike. Admittedly some statements about responsibility are found, even some true statements; but not every true statement is a definition. Once again, if we knew precisely what we were talking about, our confusion might prove avoidable.

Now, the word *responsibility* looks as if it has to do with making a response. Or, *accountability* is to give an account. A man is responsible if he must answer for what he does. Let us then define the term by saying that a person is responsible if he can be justly rewarded or punished for his deeds. This implies, of course, that he must be answerable to someone. Responsibility presupposes a superior authority that rewards and punishes. The highest authority is God. Therefore responsibility is ultimately dependent on the power and authority of God.

Is it just then for God to punish a man for deeds that God himself "determined before to be done"? Was God just in punishing Judas, Herod, Pontius Pilate, and the others? The Scriptures answer in the affirmative and explain why. Not only is God the creator of the physical universe, not only is he the governor and judge of men, he is also the moral legislator. It is his will that establishes the distinction between right and wrong, between justice and injustice; it is his will that sets the norms of righteous conduct. Most people find it easy to conceive of God as having created or established physical law by divine *fiat*. He might have created a world with a different number of planets, had he so desired. Nor does it bother some theologians to suppose that God could have made different ceremonial requirements. Instead of commanding the priests to carry the ark on their shoulders, God might have forbidden this and ordered them to put it on a cart drawn by oxen. But for some peculiar reason, people hesitate in applying the same principle of sovereignty in the sphere of ordinary ethics. Instead of recognizing God as sovereign in morals, they want to subject him to some independent, superior, ethical law – a law that satisfies their sinful opinions of what is right and wrong.

Calvin avoided any such inconsistent and un-Biblical position. In the *Institutes* (III, xxiii, 2) he says,

> how exceedingly presumptuous it is only to inquire into the causes of the divine will, which is in fact, and is justly entitled to be, the cause of everything that exists. For if it has any cause, then there must be something antecedent on which it depends; which it is impious to suppose.

For the will of God is the highest rule of justice, so that what he wills must be considered just, for this very reason, because he wills it. When it is inquired therefore why the Lord did so, the answer must be, Because he would. But if you go further and ask why he so determined, you are in search of something greater and higher than the will of God, which can never be found.

God is sovereign. Whatever he does is just, for this very reason: Because he does it. If he punishes a man, the man is justly punished; and hence the man is responsible. This answers the form of argument which runs: Whatever God does is just; eternal punishment is not just; therefore God does not so punish. If the one who argues thus means that he has received a special revelation that there is no eternal punishment, we cannot deal with him here. If, however, he is not laying claim to a special revelation of future history but to some philosophic principle which is intended to show that eternal punishment is unjust, the distinction between our positions becomes immediately obvious. Calvin has rejected the view of the universe which makes a law, whether of justice or of evolution, instead of the Lawgiver, supreme. Such a view is similar to Platonic dualism which posited a world of Ideas superior to the divine Artificer. God in such a system is finite or limited, bound to follow or obey the independent pattern. But those who hold to the sovereignty of God determine what justice is by observing what God actually does. Whatever God does is just. What he commands men to do or not to do is similarly just or unjust.

Distortions and Cautions

The arguments so far adduced are more than sufficient for the solution of the main problem. Further considerations could make the exposition more complete and might remove from inexperienced minds a number of distortions and objections that frequently present themselves. Calvinism undoubtedly stimulates many misapprehensions, although the reason for their frequency, as has already been seen in the discussion on puppets, is not a point in which Arminians can take pride. At the same time, Calvinists acknowledge that they themselves have a responsibility to forestall such misapprehensions so far as possible. The *Westminster Confession* and other Reformed creeds urge caution – not so much in opposing free will, for the Reformers were outspoken in their championship of grace in opposition to free will – but in preaching the doctrine of election and the divine decree. This does not condone those professors in Bible Departments who, supposing that they know better than God what should be revealed, demand that the doctrine of the divine decree should be suppressed in silence. But it does require that the Scriptural passages be clearly exegeted, that the doctrine should be logically integrated with the rest of God's revelation, and that at least the main objections should be squarely answered.

A recent volume, *Divine Election* by G. C. Berkouwer, is largely motivated by the pastoral concern to protect the congregation from the uncertainties and fear of a harsh presentation of election, predestination, and related themes. Professor Berkouwer is a theologian of great erudition. His volume, *The Triumph of Grace in the Theology of Karl Barth*, is a triumph of scholarship. Similarly, *The Conflict with Rome* is a masterpiece. The book under discussion also evidences a wealth of knowledge; its doctrine is unmistakably Calvinistic; and yet some of its hesitations and fears seem to be unfounded. Most of the dangers that he mentions have no doubt actually occurred, as in the writings of a certain Snethlage whom he mentions; these dangers could possibly be more common in Holland than in the United States; but so far as the present writer's experience goes, it would seem that the greater and far more common dangers are those of an opposite tendency.

For one thing, Berkouwer thinks that it is necessary to deny that Calvinism is deterministic. The word *determinism* apparently carries some evil connotation in his mind. Unfortunately Berkouwer never clearly defines *determinism*. Between the lines we may gather that determinism for him automatically makes all differences within God's predetermination relative and unimportant (180), so that preaching becomes useless (220). There are of course various types of determinism, atheistic and mechanical as well as theistic and teleological. This, however, is a poor reason for avoiding the word *determinism*. On the contrary, a uniform avoidance of this term might suggest to the congregation that the pastor does not really believe that God controls every event; and this unfortunate result would surely be more serious than any mistake arising from the word *determinism*. Sinful human nature is much more apt to deny or to circumscribe God's authority in favor of human independence than it is to exaggerate the power of God. Pastoral caution and care, therefore, lead rather in the opposite direction.

Berkouwer also cautions against ascribing absolute power to God, against asserting God's superiority to all law, and against calling his decisions arbitrary. In each case, however, there is a sense in which these terms can be used of God as well as a sense in which they are objectionable. Perhaps Occam's idea of absolute power is not correct, yet Berkouwer admits that there is no law superior to God and that in this sense God is indeed "Ex-lex." When discussing the parable of the employer who paid his laborers the same wage regardless of the time they worked, Berkouwer says that this was not "arbitrary" – it was "good." So it was; but Berkouwer's concern seems centered more on words than on their meaning.

Berkouwer also shows himself to be suspicious of the concept of causality, largely because the idea of cause tends to "a metaphysical determinism which leaves no room for variation and differences but which subsumes everything under the one causality of God" (178). This is an empty objection if ever there was one; and the discussion leaves much to be desired, because Berkouwer admits that "it is inherently difficult to give any answer that in itself would be transparent to reflective and reasonable thinking.

> *Sinful human nature is much more apt to deny or to circumscribe God's authority in favor of human independence than it is to exaggerate the power of God.*

"On the one hand, we want to maintain the freedom of God in election, and on the other hand, we want to avoid any conclusion which would make God the cause of sin and unbelief" (181).

Berkouwer, in spite of his Calvinism and his many truly fine statements of the Reformed position, is so embarrassed by his imaginary difficulties that once he even stumbles into what I take to be an historical blunder. He writes, "What Jacobs says of Calvin — that in his preaching and commentaries the election of God is repeatedly discussed, while rejection is not mentioned, can be said with as much validity of the Reformed confessions" (194). This sentence in its context seems to mean that the Reformed confessions do not even mention reprobation. This is not true; and we hope that Berkouwer intended to say something else but merely failed to express it clearly. That the ostensible meaning, however, is not true is undeniable. Earlier in this chapter a part of the *Westminster Confession* was quoted, and the reader's attention is again called to the third, fourth, and seventh sections of chapter three.

It is not by a strained analysis of the concept of causality that Berkouwer can avoid calling God the cause of sin or can contribute to the prevention of misapprehensions. There are indeed two mistaken conclusions that should be guarded against — not so much for the purpose of protecting Calvinistic congregations from anxiety and insecurity, as Berkouwer believes — but in order to save Arminians from the blunders they have fallen into. In connection with the clause, *God is the cause of sin*, something yet needs to be said about causality, and, second, something needs to be said about God's holiness.

Berkouwer had complained that the attempt to explain the divine decree in terms of causality prevented the acknowledgment of differences and variations within the divine decree and therefore eliminated these distinctions in the historical process. Even though Berkouwer admits that there are two types of causality, he still concludes that "every discussion of causality fails, must fail" (190).

The question is slightly complex. One part of it has to do with the necessity of means, or secondary or proximate causes. God does not do everything — he hardly does anything — immediately. For this reason the *Westminster Confession*, to which Berkouwer pays insufficient attention, has a phrase about secondary causation.

It is human nature, depraved human nature, to attempt to avoid responsibility for wrongdoing. In seeking to excuse himself for an evil act, a man may assign the blame to his tempter, as Adam and Eve did, or to compelling and extenuating circumstances, or to something else more remote and ultimate. The insincerity of this procedure becomes apparent when we notice that men do not try to avoid praise and honor by referring their good acts to ultimate causes. They wish to escape blame, but they are willing, only too willing, to accept compliments. The Christian view, however, is clearly expressed in David's great confession. David did not complain, I have sinned a great sin, but alas, I was born sinful and could not help it; so, do not blame me too

> *Men do not try to avoid praise and honor by referring their good acts to ultimate causes. They wish to escape blame, but they are willing, only too willing, to accept compliments.*

much. On the contrary, David said, I have sinned a great sin; and what makes it all the worse is that I was born that way; I could not help it, for I myself am evil. Repentant David placed the blame, not on his mother, nor on Adam, nor on God, even though all of these are causes in the chain of causation leading to his sin. Repentant David placed the blame on the immediate cause of his act – himself. The doctrine of creation, with its implication that there is no power independent of God, does not deny but rather establishes the existence of secondary causes. To suppose otherwise is unscriptural, and to avoid the notion of causality is illogical.

Berkouwer's contention that an original, all inclusive, universal decree of causation removes other distinctions is also untenable. He is afraid that the principle of causality would conflict with the very Scriptural position that guilt is the judicial ground of condemnation. Now, this is an important factor, a most important factor for pastoral caution. The majority of people, both inside and outside the church, are immersed in practical details, and their vision seldom rises to more general theological principles. They need the point emphasized that God condemns people for their sins. In particular, evangelistic endeavor cannot omit the fact of sin. But Calvinism does not make any such omission. Nor is there any inconsistency. The doctrines of election and reprobation do not conflict with the fact that God's punishment is visited on no one who is not a sinner. The sinner deserves his punishment because he is evil and has done evil. No innocent person suffers. To be sure, Calvinism also insists that there are no innocent persons, except Christ of course. All are dead in sin. Salvation is a free, unmerited gift. Sin alone has merited wages, and those wages are death. All this, Calvinism proclaims without compromise. There is nothing in the divine decree that is inconsistent with acknowledging sin as the judicial ground of punishment. Berkouwer's claim that the concept of cause removes particularities from the divine decree is therefore untenable.

There are admittedly other details whose discussion might obviate various misunderstandings. To consider them all, even if they were not repetitious, would require a length and minuteness incompatible with the present plan. There is, however, one extremely important topic that cannot be omitted. Does the view here defended make God the cause and author of sin? Berkouwer asks this question also, and so has everyone else.

Let it be unequivocally said that this view certainly makes God the cause of sin. God is the sole ultimate cause of everything. There is absolutely nothing independent of him. He alone is the eternal being. He alone is omnipotent. He alone is sovereign. Not only is Satan his creature, but every detail of history was eternally in his plan before the world began; and he willed that it should all come to pass. The men and angels predestined to eternal life and those foreordained to everlasting death are particularly and unchangeably designed; and their number is so certain and definite that it cannot be either increased or diminished. Election and reprobation are equally ultimate. God determined that Christ should die; he determined as well that Judas should betray him. There was never the remotest possibility that something different could have happened.

Whatever the Lord pleases he does, in Heaven and in Earth [*Psalm* 135:6].

All the inhabitants of the Earth are reputed as nothing; he does according to his will in the army of Heaven and among the inhabitants of the Earth. No one can restrain his hand or say to him, "What have you done?" [*Daniel* 4:35].

I form the light and create darkness, I make peace and create evil; I, the Lord, do all these things [*Isaiah* 45:7].

The Lord has made all things for himself, yes, even the wicked for the day of evil [*Proverbs* 16:4].

You will say to me then, "Why does he still find fault? For who has resisted his will?" But indeed, O man, who are you to reply against God?...Does not the potter have power over the clay, from the same lump to make one vessel for honor and another for dishonor? [*Romans* 9:19-21].

Therefore consider the goodness and severity of God [*Romans* 11:22].

One is permitted to ask, however, whether the phrase "cause of sin" is the equivalent of the phrase "author of sin." Is the latter phrase used to deny God's universal causality? Obviously not, for the same people who affirm causality deny the authorship. They must have intended a difference. An illustration is close at hand. God is not the author of this book, as the Arminians would be the first to admit; but he is its ultimate cause as the Bible teaches. Yet I am the author. Authorship therefore is one kind of cause, but there are other kinds. The author of a book is its immediate cause; God is its ultimate cause.

This distinction between first and secondary causation – explicitly maintained in the *Westminster Confession* – has not always been appreciated, even by those who are in general agreement. John Gill, for example, who is so excellent on so much, failed to grasp the distinction between the immediate author and the ultimate cause. For this reason there are some faulty passages in his otherwise fine work. Such is the difficulty of the problem and so confused are the discussions from the time of the patristics to the present day, that some of the best Calvinists have not extricated themselves completely from scholastic errors. Not only Berkouwer, but even Jonathan Edwards, in spite of Calvin, still spoke about God's permission of sin.

When, accordingly, the discussion comes to God's being the author of sin, one must understand the question to be, Is God the immediate cause of sin? Or, more clearly, Does God commit sin? This is a question concerning God's holiness. Now, it should be evident that God no more commits sin than he is writing these words. Although the betrayal of Christ was foreordained from eternity as a means of effecting the atonement, it was Judas, not God, who betrayed Christ. The

> *"I form the light and create darkness, I make peace and create evil; I, the Lord, do all these things."*
> *– Isaiah 45:7*

secondary causes in history are not eliminated by divine causality, but rather they are made certain. And the acts of these secondary causes, whether they be righteous acts or sinful acts, are to be immediately referred to the agents; and it is these agents who are responsible.

God is neither responsible nor sinful, even though he is the only ultimate cause of everything. He is not sinful because in the first place whatever God does is just and right. It is just and right simply in virtue of the fact that he does it. Justice or righteousness is not a standard external to God to which God is obligated to submit. Righteousness is what God does. Since God caused Judas to betray Christ, this causal act is righteous and not sinful. By definition God cannot sin. At this point it must be particularly pointed out that God's causing a man to sin is not sin. There is no law, superior to God, which forbids him to decree sinful acts. Sin presupposes a law, for sin is lawlessness. Sin is any want of conformity unto or transgression of the law of God. But God is "Ex-lex."

True it is that if a man, a created being, should cause or try to cause another man to sin, this attempt would be sinful. The reason is plain. The relation of one man to another is entirely different from the relation of God to any man. God is the creator; man is a creature. And the relation of a man to the law is equally different from the relation of God to the law. What holds in the one situation does not hold in the other. God has absolute and unlimited rights over all created things. Of the same lump he can make one vessel for honor and another for dishonor. The clay has no claims on the potter. Among men, on the contrary, rights are limited.

The idea that God is above law can be explained in another particular. The laws that God imposes on men do not apply to the divine nature. They are applicable only to human conditions. For example, God cannot steal, not only because whatever he does is right, but also because he owns everything: There is no one to steal from. Thus the law that defines sin envisages human conditions and has no relevance to a sovereign Creator.

As God cannot sin, so in the next place, God is not responsible for sin, even though he decrees it. Perhaps it would be well, before we conclude, to give a little more Scriptural evidence that God indeed decrees and causes sin. *2 Chronicles* 18:20-22 read: "Then a spirit came forward and stood before the Lord, and said, 'I will persuade him.' The Lord said to him, 'In what way?' So he said, 'I will go out and be a lying spirit in the mouth of all his prophets.' And the Lord said, 'You shall persuade him and also prevail; go out and do so.' Now, therefore, look! The Lord has put a lying spirit in the mouth of these prophets of yours, and the Lord has declared disaster against you." This passage definitely says that the Lord caused the prophets to lie. Other similar passages ought easily to come to one's remembrance. But that God is not responsible for the sin he causes is a conclusion closely connected with the preceding argument.

Another aspect of the human conditions presupposed by the laws

God imposes on man is that they carry with them a penalty that cannot be inflicted on God. Man is responsible because God calls him to account; man is responsible because the supreme power can punish him for disobedience. God, on the contrary, cannot be responsible for the plain reason that there is no power superior to him; no greater being can hold him accountable; no one can punish him; there is no one to whom God is responsible; there are no laws which he could disobey. The sinner, therefore, and not God, is responsible; the sinner alone is the author of sin. Man has no free will, for salvation is purely of grace; and God is sovereign.

Deo Soli Gloria

> I am the Lord, and there is no other; there is no God besides me.... I form the light and create darkness, I make peace and create evil; I, the Lord, do all these things.... Woe to him who strives with his Maker!... Shall the clay say to him who forms it, "What are you making?"... Thus says the Lord, the Holy One of Israel,... I have made the Earth, and created man on it. It was I – my hands that stretched out the heavens, and all their host I have commanded.... Oh, the depth of the riches both of the wisdom and knowledge of God! How unsearchable are his judgments and his ways past finding out!... For of him and through him and to him are all things, to whom be glory forever. Amen.

The sinner, therefore, and not God, is responsible; the sinner alone is the author of sin. Man has no free will, for salvation is purely of grace; and God is sovereign.

Scripture Index

Acts
    4:27-28 *18*
    4:28 *31*
    7:2 *24*
    19:44 *24*
    22:1 *24*

2 Chronicles
    18:20-22 *40*

Daniel
    4:35 *39*

Ephesians
    1:11 *27*

Isaiah
    8:16, 18 *24*
    45:7 *39*

Luke
    12:47 *33*

Matthew
    12:27 *24*
    23:37 *23*

Proverbs
    16:4 *39*
    22:6 *33*

Psalms
    65:4 *33*
    135:6 *39*

Romans
    1 *33*
    5:17 *33*
    9:19-21 *39*
    11:22 *39*

INDEX

ability 14-15
Abraham 28
accountability 34
action(s) 11, 15, 18, 29, 32, 34
acts 37, 40
Adam 11, 14, 22, 33, 37-38
adoption 23
angels 14, 21, 22, 38
apostles 19
Aristotle 10-11
ark 34
Arminianism 23
Arminians 16, 18
Arminius 22
assurance 23
astronomy 33
atonement 39
Augustine 10-15, 17, 27, 30; Works: *City of God* 13-14; *Free Will* 13
author of sin 22, 38-39, 41
authority 34, 36

Barnabas 19
Baylis, Charles A. 11
Bede 20
being 13
believe 21
benevolence 8
Berkouwer, G. C. 35-38; Works: *The Conflict with Rome* 36; *Divine Election* 35; *The Triumph of Grace in the Theology of Karl Barth*, 36
Bible 7, 12, 14, 17, 23, 28, 39

blame 11, 37
blasphemy 22
Bloody Mary 21
Bondage of the Will, The (Luther) 21
Bradwardine, Thomas 20
Bucer, Martin 21

calamities 10
Calvin, John 12, 17, 21, 27, 34-35, 37; Works: *Institutes of the Christian Religion* 17, 34-35
Calvinism 9, 18-19, 22-24, 28-29, 31-32, 35, 37-38; five points of 18, 21
Calvinists 18
causality 10, 16, 21, 25, 32, 36-38, 40
Cause of God and Truth, The (Gill) 14-15, 23, 29
character 11, 16
choice(s) 15-16, 18, 27, 30-32
Christian college 18
Christianity 10-12, 22, 25
Chrysippus 30
church 20
circumstances 37
City of God (Augustine) 13-14
Clark, Gordon H. 8; Works: *Religion, Reason, and Revelation* 8
Clement of Rome 19
coaction 31
commands 28
compliments 37
compulsion 31
condemnation 38

Confession of 1508 (Waldensians) 20
confessions 37
Conflict in Religious Thought (Harkness) 27
Conflict with Rome, The (Berkouwer) 36
consistency 9
consolation 23
contradiction(s) 26, 28
corruption 30
cosmological argument 28
Council of Trent 21
Cranmer, Thomas 21
creation 26-27, 38
creature 21
crucifixion 27-28

David 37-38
death 9, 33-34, 38
decisions 11, 13
decree 22, 28-29, 37-38
decree of God 22
decrees 27
decretive will 28
deeds 34
deficient causes 10, 12
definition(s) 9, 24, 28
Demiurge 10
demon 12
determinism 11, 17-18, 26-28, 30, 33-35, 36
diligence 23
disaster 40
disease 10
disobedience 9, 34, 41
divine decree(s) 30, 35, 37-38
Divine Election (Berkouwer) 35
divine will 34
dualism 10, 13, 35
Duke University 11

Earth 39
education 33
Edwards, Jonathan 26, 39; *Works: Miscellaneous Observations* 26
effectual calling 22-23
efficient cause 10
elect 14, 20, 22, 23
election 22-24, 35-39
emotions 12
Epistle to the Ephesians (Ignatius) 20

Epistle to the Romans (Ignatius) 20
Erasmus 21
eternal punishment 35
eternity 22
ethics 11, 34
Eve 37
everlasting life 22
evil 7, 8, 11-12, 41
evolution 35
Ex-lex 36, 40
exegesis 24-25

faith 22-23
fall 14
fallacy 7
false piety 26
fate 27, 30
fatigue 32
finite god 12, 18
five points of Calvinism 18, 21
force 31
foreknowledge 21, 25
foreordination 18, 21
free agency 31
free choice 22
free moral agent 27
free will 7, 12-17, 17, 20-27, 29-33, 35, 41
Free Will (Augustine) 13
future 10, 22, 25-26

Garvin, Lucius 11
Gentiles 33
Gibson, Richard 22
Gill, John 14-15, 23-25, 29-31, 39; *Works: The Cause of God and Truth* 14-15, 23, 29
glorification 14
glory 11, 20
God 7-9, 11-12, 14, 16-18, 21-22, 24, 26-27, 31, 33, 38, 40; authority of 34, 36; decree of 22, 28-30, 35, 37-38; existence of 10; Father 20; freedom of 37; holiness of 37, 39; Holy Spirit 23; image of 33; immutability of 30; omnipotence of 7, 10, 12, 25-27, 38; power of 33-34, 36, 38; providence of 29; revealed will of 28; secret will of 28; sovereignty of 8, 29, 35, 38, 41; will of 22, 27-29, 34-35; *see also* Jesus Christ
good and evil 8

Index

good works 22
Gospel 19, 20-21, 23
Gottschalk 20
grace 13, 16, 20-22, 31, 33, 35, 41
grades of being 13
guilt 34, 38

Hackett, Stuart C. 28-29; *Works: The Resurrection of Theism* 29
Hamilton, Patrick 21
Harkness, Georgia 12, 27; *Works: Conflict in Religious Thought* 27
Heaven 14, 30, 39
heresy 21
Herod 27, 34
Heylin, Peter 21
Hincmar, Bishop 20
Historic Proof of the Doctrinal Calvinism of the Church of England (Toplady) 19
history 9, 10, 38, 40
Hobbes, Thomas 30
holiness 26, 37, 39
Holy Spirit 23
human nature 36
humility 23
Hus, Jan 20
hyper-Calvinism 29

Ignatius 20; *Works: Epistle to the Ephesians* 20; *Epistle to the Romans* 20
ignorance 18, 21, 32-33
image of God 33
immutability 30
imputation 34
inconsistency 25
indeterminism 11
inducements 15-16
inevitability 14, 18
injustice 10, 34
innate knowledge 33
Institutes of the Christian Religion (Calvin) 17, 34-35
intelligence 7
Introduction to the Philosophy of Religion, An (Patterson) 11
irresistible grace 19
Isaac 28
Islam 27

James (archbishop of St. Andrews) 21
jealousy 33
Jerusalem 23, 24
Jesus Christ 13, 15-16, 18, 24; atonement of 39-40; crucifixion 27-28; death of 39; election in 22; human nature of 14; innocence of 38
Jews 20, 27-28
Judas Iscariot 18, 31, 34, 39, 39-40
justice 23, 34-35, 40
justification 21, 23

knowledge 27, 33, 41
Knox, John 21

Lactantius 10
Latimer 21
law 28, 36, 40
law of God 30, 40
lawlessness 40
liberals 11
liberty 14-15
limited atonement 19
love 11
Lucifer 21
Luther, Martin 21, 31, 33; *Works: The Bondage of the Will* 21
Lutherans 21
lying spirit 40

man 21
Manichaeanism 13
mankind 24
man's will 29
Mary, Bloody 21
means 22
mechanical determinism 30
Melanchthon, Phillip 21
Menardus 19
mercy 23
Middle Ages 12, 19-20
Mill, John Stuart 12
Milton, John 9; *Works: Paradise Lost* 9
mind 31
Miscellaneous Observations (Edwards) 26
mistakes 25
Mohammedanism 27
Montague, William Pepperell 12

Moon 30
moral law 8, 28
morality 26, 28
Moses 17
Mothershead, John L. 11
motion 10
motives 15-16
murder 28
mysteries 26

natural liberty 29-31
necessity 14,-15, 17, 21, 29, 30-32; of coaction 30; of compulsion 31; of force 30; of immutability 30; of infallible certainty 31; of nature 30
non posse non peccare 14
non posse peccare 14
non-being 13

obedience 34
observation 26
Occam 36
omnipotence 7, 10, 11, 12, 25-27, 38
omniscience 25-26, 33

pain 10
pantheism 7
Paradise Lost (Milton) 9
paradox 17
past 10
patristics 39
Patterson, Robert Leet 11, 16; Works: *An Introduction to the Philosophy of Religion* 11
Paul 27
peace 41
Pelagius 11, 20-21
perdition 20
permission 16-17, 25, 39
perseverance 22
Pharisees 24
philosophy 15, 26
physical law 34
physiology 32-33
planets 34
Plato 10, 12; Works: *The Republic* 10
polytheism 7
Pontius Pilate 18, 27, 34
pope 22

posse non peccare 14
power 16, 19-20, 23, 33, 34, 36, 38
praise 11, 23, 37
preaching 36, 37
preceptive will 28
precepts 28
predestination 18, 20-21, 23, 27, 36
predetermination 18
predictions 26
Presbyterians 29
prescience 17, 21
presuppositionalism 28
priests 34
problem of evil 7-9, 16, 17, 24
promises 11
prophecy 18
prophets 23-24, 40
Protestantism 30
providence 29
proximate causes 37
psychological determinism 30
psychology 33
punishments 11
puppets 28-32, 35
Puritans 29, 32
purpose(s) 7, 22

redemption 14, 18, 22, 23-24
Reformation 17, 19-22
Reformation Principles, The 29
Reformed Presbyterian Church 29
Reformers 19, 35
Religion, Reason, and Revelation (Clark) 8
Remigus 20
repentance 19
reprobate 17, 20
reprobation 23-24, 37-39
Republic (Plato) 10
responsibility 8, 11, 16, 18, 26-28, 30, 33-35, 37, 41
Resurrection of Theism, The (Hackett) 29
retributive punishment 11
revealed will of God 28
revelation 35
reverence 23
Ridley 21
right and wrong 34
righteousness 40

Index

rights 40
Rock of Ages (Toplady) 19
rulers 24

saints 14, 29
salvation 21, 23, 38, 41
sanctification 23
Sanhedrin 24
sanitation 27
Satan 17, 38
Scheme of Christian and Philosophical Necessity Asserted, The (Toplady) 31
scientific theories 24
Scotland 21
scribes 24
Scriptures 18, 33
second causes 22, 38-40
secret police 9
secret will of God 28
secularism 9
secularists 12
semi-Pelagianism 22
Sihon 17
sin 7, 11, 13, 15-16, 21, 23, 26, 30, 33-34, 37, 40; author of 38-39, 41; cause of 38-39
Smithfield 22
Snethlage 36
Socrates 15
souls 13
sovereignty 18, 29, 34-35, 38, 41
Space (Platonic) 10
special revelation 35
stars 30
stealing 27
Stoicism 30
suasion 20
suffering 7
Sun 30
Synod of Dordt 21-22

Ten Commandments 28
theism 28
theodicy 23

theology 27
Thomas Aquinas 12
threats 11
Timaeus (Plato) 10
Toplady, Augustus 19-21, 30-31; *Works: Historic Proof of the Doctrinal Calvinism of the Church of England* 19; *Rock of Ages* 19; *The Scheme of Christian and Philosophical Necessity Asserted* 31; *The Works of Augustus Toplady* 19-21
torture 9, 20
Triumph of Grace in the Theology of Karl Barth, The (Berkouwer) 36
Tyndal, William 21

unbelief 37
unconditional election 18
universe 26
Unmoved Mover 10

variety 13
Voltaire 10, 16

Waldensians 20
weather 32
Westminster Assembly 22
Westminster Confession of Faith 9, 22-23, 29, 31, 34-35, 37, 39
Westminster Shorter Catechism 29
Whitby 24, 25
will of God 17, 19, 21, 23, 27-29, 34
Woodman, Richard 21
Word of God 22
Works of Augustus Toplady, The 19-21
world of Ideas 35
worldview 9
wrath 11, 17, 23
Wycliffe, John 20-21

Zanchius, Jerome 21
Zoroaster 11-12
Zoroastrianism 10
Zwingli 21

The Crisis of Our Time

Historians have christened the thirteenth century the Age of Faith and termed the eighteenth century the Age of Reason. The present age has been called many things: the Atomic Age, the Age of Inflation, the Age of the Tyrant, the Age of Aquarius; but it deserves one name more than the others: the Age of Irrationalism. Contemporary secular intellectuals are anti-intellectual. Contemporary philosophers are anti-philosophy. Contemporary theologians are anti-theology.

In past centuries, secular philosophers have generally believed that knowledge is possible to man. Consequently they expended a great deal of thought and effort trying to justify knowledge. In the twentieth century, however, the optimism of the secular philosophers all but disappeared. They despaired of knowledge.

Like their secular counterparts, the great theologians and doctors of the church taught that knowledge is possible to man. Yet the theologians of the present age also repudiated that belief. They too despaired of knowledge. This radical skepticism has penetrated our entire culture, from television to music to literature. *The Christian at the beginning of the twenty-first century is confronted with an overwhelming cultural consensus – sometimes stated explicitly but most often implicitly: Man does not and cannot know anything truly.*

What does this have to do with Christianity? Simply this: If man can know nothing truly, man can truly know nothing. We cannot know that the Bible is the Word of God, that Christ died for his people, or that Christ is alive today at the right hand of the Father. Unless knowledge is possible, Christianity is nonsensical, for it claims to be knowledge. What is at stake at the beginning of the twenty-first century is not simply a single doctrine, such as the virgin birth, or the existence of Hell, as important as those doctrines may be, but the whole of Christianity itself. If knowledge is not possible to man, it is worse than silly to argue points of doctrine – it is insane.

The irrationalism of the present age is so thoroughgoing and pervasive that even the Remnant – the segment of the professing church that remains faithful – has accepted much of it, frequently without even being aware of what it is accepting. In some religious circles this irrationalism has become synonymous with piety and humility, and those who oppose it are denounced as rationalists, as though to be logical were a sin. Our contemporary anti-theologians make a contradiction and call it a Mystery. The faithful ask for truth and are given Paradox and Antinomy. If any balk at swallowing the absurdities of the anti-theologians who teach in the seminaries or have graduated from the seminaries, they are frequently marked as heretics or schismatics who seek to act independently of God.

There is no greater threat facing the church of Christ at this moment than the irrationalism that now controls our entire culture. Totalitarianism, guilty of tens of millions of murders – including those of millions of Christians – is to be feared, but not nearly so much as the idea that we do not and cannot know the literal truth. Hedonism, the popular philosophy of America, is not to be feared so much as the belief that logic – that "mere human logic," to use the religious irrationalists' own phrase – is futile. The attacks on truth, on knowledge, on propositional revelation, on the intellect, on words, and on logic are renewed daily. But note well: The misologists – the haters of logic – use logic to demonstrate the futility of using logic. The anti-intellectuals construct intricate intellectual arguments to prove the insufficiency of the intellect. Those who deny the competence of words to express thought use words to express their thoughts. The proponents of poetry, myth, metaphor, and analogy argue for their theories by using literal prose, whose competence – even whose possibility – they deny. The anti-theologians use the revealed Word of God to show that there can be no revealed Word of God – or that if there could, it would remain impenetrable darkness and Mystery to our finite minds.

Nonsense Has Come

Is it any wonder that the world is grasping at straws – the straws of experientialism, mysticism, and drugs? After all, if people are told that the Bible contains insoluble mysteries, then is not a flight into mysticism to be expected? On what grounds can it be condemned? Certainly not on logical grounds or Biblical grounds, if logic is futile and the Bible unknowable. Moreover, if it cannot be condemned on logical or Biblical grounds, it cannot be condemned at all. If people are going to have a religion of the mysterious, they will not adopt Christianity: They will have a genuine mystery religion. The popularity of mysticism, drugs, and religious experience is the logical consequence of the irrationalism of the present age. There can and will be no Christian reformation – and no restoration of a free society – unless and until the irrationalism of the age is totally repudiated by Christians.

The Church Defenseless

Yet how shall they do it? The official spokesmen for Christianity have been fatally infected with irrationalism. The seminaries, which annually train thousands of men to teach millions of Christians, are the finishing schools of irrationalism, completing the job begun by the government schools and colleges. Most of the pulpits of the conservative churches (we are not speaking of the obviously apostate churches) are occupied by graduates of the anti-theological schools. These products of modern anti-theological education, when asked to give a reason for the hope that is in them, can generally respond with only the intellectual analogue of a shrug – a mumble about Mystery. They have not grasped – and therefore cannot teach those for whom they are responsible – the first truth: "And you shall know the truth." Many, in fact, explicitly contradict Christ, saying that, at best, we possess only "pointers" to the truth, or something "similar" to the truth, a mere analogy. Is the impotence of the Christian church a puzzle? Is the fascination with Pentecostalism, faith healing, Eastern Orthodoxy, and Roman Catholicism – all sensate and anti-intellectual religions – among members of Christian churches an enigma? Not when one understands the pious nonsense that is purveyed in the name of God in the religious colleges and seminaries.

The Trinity Foundation

The creators of The Trinity Foundation firmly believe that theology is too important to be left to the licensed theologians – the graduates of the schools of theology. They have created The Trinity Foundation for the express purpose of teaching believers all that the Scriptures contain –

not warmed over, baptized, Antichristian philosophies. Each member of the board of directors of The Trinity Foundation has signed this oath: "I believe that the Bible alone and the Bible in its entirety is the Word of God and, therefore, inerrant in the autographs. I believe that the system of truth presented in the Bible is best summarized in the *Westminster Confession of Faith*. So help me God."

The ministry of The Trinity Foundation is the presentation of the system of truth taught in Scripture as clearly and as completely as possible. We do not regard obscurity as a virtue, nor confusion as a sign of spirituality. Confusion, like all error, is sin, and teaching that confusion is all that Christians can hope for is doubly sin.

The presentation of the truth of Scripture necessarily involves the rejection of error. The Foundation has exposed and will continue to expose the irrationalism of the present age, whether its current spokesman be an existentialist philosopher or a professed Reformed theologian. We oppose anti-intellectualism, whether it be espoused by a Neo-orthodox theologian or a fundamentalist evangelist. We reject misology, whether it be on the lips of a Neo-evangelical or those of a Roman Catholic Charismatic. We repudiate agnosticism, whether it be secular or religious. To each error we bring the brilliant light of Scripture, proving all things, and holding fast to that which is true.

The Primacy of Theory

The ministry of The Trinity Foundation is not a "practical" ministry. If you are a pastor, we will not enlighten you on how to organize an ecumenical prayer meeting in your community or how to double church attendance in a year. If you are a homemaker, you will have to read elsewhere to find out how to become a total woman. If you are a businessman, we will not tell you how to develop a social conscience. The professing church is drowning in such "practical" advice.

The Trinity Foundation is unapologetically theoretical in its outlook, believing that theory without practice is dead, and that practice without theory is blind. The trouble with the professing church is not primarily in its practice, but in its theory. Churchgoers and teachers do not know, and many do not even care to know, the doctrines of Scripture. Doctrine is intellectual, and churchgoers and teachers are generally anti-intellectual. Doctrine is ivory tower philosophy, and they scorn ivory towers. The ivory tower, however, is the control tower of a civilization. It is a fundamental, theoretical mistake of the "practical" men to think that they can be merely practical, for practice is always the practice of some theory. The relationship between theory and practice is the relationship between cause and effect. If a person believes correct theory, his practice will tend to be correct. The practice of contemporary Christians is immoral because it is the practice of false theories. It is a major theoretical mistake of the "practical" men to think that they can ignore the ivory towers of the philosophers and theologians as irrelevant to their lives. Every action that "practical" men take is governed by the thinking that has occurred in some ivory tower – whether that tower be the British Museum; the Academy; a home in Basel, Switzerland; or a tent in Israel.

In Understanding Be Men

It is the first duty of the Christian to understand correct theory – correct doctrine – and thereby implement correct practice. This order – first theory, then practice – is both logical and Biblical. It is, for example, exhibited in Paul's *Epistle to the Romans,* in which he spends the first eleven chapters expounding theory and the last five discussing practice. The contemporary teachers of Christians have not only reversed the Biblical order, they have inverted the Pauline emphasis on theory and practice. The virtually complete failure of the teachers of the professing church to instruct believers in correct doctrine is the cause of the misconduct and spiritual and cultural impotence of Christians. The church's lack of power is the result of its lack of truth. The *Gospel* is the power of God, not religious experiences or personal relationships. The church has no power because it has abandoned the Gospel, the good news, for a religion of experientialism. Twentieth-first-century American churchgoers are children carried about by every wind of doctrine, not knowing what they believe, or even if they believe anything for certain.

The chief purpose of The Trinity Foundation is to counteract the irrationalism of the age and to expose the errors of the teachers of the church. Our emphasis – on the Bible as the sole source of knowledge, on the primacy of truth, on the supreme importance of correct doctrine, and on the necessity for systematic and logical thinking – is almost unique in Christendom. To the extent that the church survives – and she will survive and flourish – it will be because of her increasing acceptance of these basic ideas and their logical implications.

We believe that The Trinity Foundation is filling a vacuum in Christendom. We are saying that Christianity is intellectually defensible – that, in fact, it is the only intellectually defensible system of thought. We are saying that God has made the wisdom of this world – whether that wisdom be called science, religion, philosophy, or common sense – foolishness. We are appealing to all Christians who have not conceded defeat in the intellectual battle with the world to join us in our efforts to raise a standard to which all men of sound mind can repair.

The love of truth, of God's Word, has all but disappeared in our time. We are committed to and pray for a great instauration. But though we may not see this reformation in our lifetimes, we believe it is our duty to present the whole counsel of God, because Christ has commanded it. The results of our teaching are in God's hands, not ours. Whatever those results, his Word is never taught in vain, but always accomplishes the result that he intended it to accomplish. Professor Gordon H. Clark has stated our view well:

> There have been times in the history of God's people, for example, in the days of Jeremiah, when refreshing grace and widespread revival were not to be expected: The time was one of chastisement. If this twentieth century is of a similar nature, individual Christians here and there can find comfort and strength in a study of God's Word. But if God has decreed happier days for us, and if we may expect a world-shaking and genuine spiritual awakening, then it is the author's belief that a zeal for souls, however necessary, is not the sufficient condition. Have there not been devout saints in every age, numerous enough to carry on a revival? Twelve such persons are plenty. What distinguishes the arid ages from the period of the Reformation, when nations were moved as they had not been since Paul preached in Ephesus, Corinth, and Rome, is the latter's fullness of knowledge of God's Word. To echo an early Reformation thought, when the ploughman and the garage attendant know the Bible as well as the theologian does, and know it better than some contemporary theologians, then the desired awakening shall have already occurred.

In addition to publishing books, the Foundation publishes a monthly newsletter, *The Trinity Review*. Subscriptions to *The Review* are free to U.S. addresses; please write to the address on the order form to become a subscriber. If you would like further information or would like to join us in our work, please let us know.

The Trinity Foundation is a non-profit foundation, tax exempt under section 501 (c)(3) of the Internal Revenue Code of 1954. You can help us disseminate the Word of God through your tax-deductible contributions to the Foundation.

JOHN W. ROBBINS

Intellectual Ammunition

The Trinity Foundation is committed to bringing every philosophical and theological thought captive to Christ. The books listed below are designed to accomplish that goal. They are written with two subordinate purposes: (1) to demolish all non-Christian claims to knowledge; and (2) to build a system of truth based upon the Bible alone.

Philosophy

Ancient Philosophy
Gordon H. Clark   Trade paperback $24.95

This book covers the thousand years from the Pre-Socratics to Plotinus. It represents some of the early work of Dr. Clark – the work that made his academic reputation. It is an excellent college text.

Behaviorism and Christianity
Gordon H. Clark   Trade paperback $5.95

Behaviorism is a critique of both secular and religious behaviorists. It includes chapters on John Watson, Edgar S. Singer, Jr., Gilbert Ryle, B. F. Skinner, and Donald MacKay. Clark's refutation of behaviorism and his argument for a Christian doctrine of man are unanswerable.

A Christian Philosophy of Education   Hardback $18.95
Gordon H. Clark   Trade paperback $12.95

The first edition of this book was published in 1946. It sparked the contemporary interest in Christian schools. In the 1970s, Dr. Clark thoroughly revised and updated it, and it is needed now more than ever. Its chapters include: The Need for a World-View; The Christian World-View; The Alternative to Christian Theism; Neutrality; Ethics; The Christian Philosophy of Education; Academic Matters; and Kindergarten to University. Three appendices are included: The Relationship of Public Education to Christianity; A Protestant World-View; and Art and the Gospel.

A Christian View of Men and Things   Hardback $29.95
Gordon H. Clark   Trade paperback $14.95

No other book achieves what *A Christian View* does: the presentation of Christianity as it applies to history, politics, ethics, science, religion, and epistemology. Dr. Clark's command of both worldly philosophy and Scripture is evident on every page, and the result is a breathtaking and invigorating challenge to the wisdom of this world.

Clark Speaks from the Grave
Gordon H. Clark   Trade paperback $3.95
   Dr. Clark chides some of his critics for their failure to defend Christianity competently. *Clark Speaks* is a stimulating and illuminating discussion of the errors of contemporary apologists.

Ecclesiastical Megalomania: The Economic and Political Thought of the Roman Catholic Church
John W. Robbins   Hardback $21.95
   This detailed and thorough analysis and critique of the social teaching of the Roman Church-State is the only such book available by a Christian economist and political philosopher. The book's conclusions reveal the Roman Church-State to be an advocate of its own brand of faith-based fascism. *Ecclesiastical Megalomania* includes the complete text of the *Donation of Constantine* and Lorenzo Valla's exposé of the hoax.

Education, Christianity, and the State
J. Gresham Machen   Trade paperback $10.95
   Machen was one of the foremost educators, theologians, and defenders of Christianity in the twentieth century. The author of several scholarly books, Machen saw clearly that if Christianity is to survive and flourish, a system of Christian schools must be established. This collection of essays and speeches captures his thoughts on education over nearly three decades.

Essays on Ethics and Politics
Gordon H. Clark   Trade paperback $10.95
   Dr. Clark's essays, written over the course of five decades, are a major statement of Christian ethics.

Gordon H. Clark: Personal Recollections
John W. Robbins, editor   Trade paperback $6.95
   Friends of Dr. Clark have written their recollections of the man. Contributors include family members, colleagues, students, and friends such as Harold Lindsell, Carl Henry, Ronald Nash, and Anna Marie Hager.

Historiography: Secular and Religious
Gordon H. Clark   Trade paperback $13.95
   In this masterful work, Dr. Clark applies his philosophy to the writing of history, examining all the major schools of historiography.

An Introduction to Christian Philosophy
Gordon H. Clark   Trade paperback $8.95
   In 1966 Dr. Clark delivered three lectures on philosophy at Wheaton College. In these lectures he criticizes secular philosophy and launches a philosophical revolution in the name of Christ.

Intellectual Ammunition

Language and Theology
Gordon H. Clark   Trade paperback $9.95

There were two main currents in twentieth-century philosophy – language philosophy and existentialism. Both were hostile to Christianity. Dr. Clark disposes of language philosophy in this brilliant critique of Bertrand Russell, Ludwig Wittgenstein, Rudolf Carnap, A. J. Ayer, Langdon Gilkey, and many others.

Logic   Hardback $16.95
Gordon H. Clark   Trade paperback $10.95

Written as a textbook for Christian schools, *Logic* is another unique book from Dr. Clark's pen. His presentation of the laws of thought, which must be followed if Scripture is to be understood correctly, and which are found in Scripture itself, is both clear and thorough. *Logic* is an indispensable book for the thinking Christian.

Lord God of Truth, Concerning the Teacher
Gordon H. Clark and
Aurelius Augustine   Trade paperback $7.95

This essay by Dr. Clark summarizes many of the most telling arguments against empiricism and defends the Biblical teaching that we know God and truth immediately. The dialogue by Augustine is a refutation of empirical language philosophy.

The Philosophy of Science and Belief in God
Gordon H. Clark   Trade paperback $8.95

In opposing the contemporary idolatry of science, Dr. Clark analyzes three major aspects of science: the problem of motion, Newtonian science, and modern theories of physics. His conclusion is that science, while it may be useful, is always false; and he demonstrates its falsity in numerous ways. Since science is always false, it can offer no alternative to the Bible and Christianity.

Religion, Reason and Revelation
Gordon H. Clark   Trade paperback $10.95

One of Dr. Clark's apologetical masterpieces, *Religion, Reason and Revelation* has been praised for the clarity of its thought and language. It includes these chapters: Is Christianity a Religion? Faith and Reason; Inspiration and Language; Revelation and Morality; and God and Evil. It is must reading for all serious Christians.

The Scripturalism of Gordon H. Clark
W. Gary Crampton   Trade paperback $9.95

Dr. Crampton has written an introduction to the philosophy of Gordon H. Clark that is helpful to both beginners and advanced students of theology. This book includes a bibliography of Dr. Clark's works.

Thales to Dewey:
A History of Philosophy   Hardback $29.95
Gordon H. Clark   Trade paperback $21.95

This is the best one-volume history of philosophy in print.

Three Types of Religious Philosophy
Gordon H. Clark   Trade paperback $6.95

 In this book on apologetics, Dr. Clark examines empiricism, rationalism, dogmatism, and contemporary irrationalism, which does not rise to the level of philosophy. He offers an answer to the question, "How can Christianity be defended before the world?"

William James and John Dewey
Gordon H. Clark   Trade paperback $8.95

 William James and John Dewey are two of the most influential philosophers America has produced. Their philosophies of instrumentalism and pragmatism are hostile to Christianity, and Dr. Clark demolishes their arguments.

Without A Prayer: Ayn Rand and the Close of Her System
John W. Robbins   Hardback $27.95

 Ayn Rand has been a best-selling author since 1957. *Without A Prayer* discusses Objectivism's epistemology, theology, ethics, and politics in detail. Appendices include analyses of books by Leonard Peikoff and David Kelley, as well as several essays on Christianity and philosophy.

Theology

Against the Churches: The Trinity Review 1989-1998
John W. Robbins, editor   Oversize hardback $39.95

 This is the second volume of essays from *The Trinity Review*, covering its second ten years, 1989-1998. This volume, like the first, is fully indexed and is very useful in research and in the classroom. Authors include: Gordon Clark, John Robbins, Charles Hodge, J. C. Ryle, Horatius Bonar, and Robert L. Dabney.

Against the World: The Trinity Review 1978-1988
John W. Robbins, editor   Oversize hardback $34.95

 This is a clothbound collection of the essays published in *The Trinity Review* from 1978 to 1988, 70 in all. It is a valuable source of information and arguments explaining and defending Christianity.

The Atonement
Gordon H. Clark   Trade paperback $8.95

 In *The Atonement,* Dr. Clark discusses the covenants, the virgin birth and incarnation, federal headship and representation, the relationship between God's sovereignty and justice, and much more. He analyzes traditional views of the atonement and criticizes them in the light of Scripture alone.

The Biblical Doctrine of Man
Gordon H. Clark   Trade paperback $6.95

 Is man soul and body or soul, spirit, and body? What is the image of God? Is Adam's sin imputed to his children? Is evolution true? Are men totally depraved? What is the heart? These are some of the questions discussed and answered from Scripture in this book.

Intellectual Ammunition

By Scripture Alone
W. Gary Crampton   Trade paperback $12.95
   This is a clear and thorough explanation of the Scriptural doctrine of Scripture and a refutation of the recent Romanist attack on Scripture as the Word of God.

The Changing of the Guard
Mark W. Karlberg   Trade paperback $3.95
   This essay is a critical discussion of Westminster Seminary's anti-Reformational and un-Biblical teaching on the doctrine of justification. Dr. Karlberg exposes the doctrine of justification by faith and works — not *sola fide* — taught at Westminster Seminary for the past 25 years, by Professors Norman Shepherd, Richard Gaffin, John Frame, and others.

The Church Effeminate
John W. Robbins, editor   Hardback $29.95
   This is a collection of 39 essays by the best theologians of the church on the doctrine of the church: Martin Luther, John Calvin, Benjamin Warfield, Gordon Clark, J. C. Ryle, and many more. The essays cover the structure, function, and purpose of the church.

The Clark-Van Til Controversy
Herman Hoeksema   Trade paperback $7.95
   This collection of essays by the founder of the Protestant Reformed Churches — essays written at the time of the Clark-Van Til controversy in the 1940s — is one of the best commentaries on those events in print.

A Companion to The Current Justification Controversy
John W. Robbins   Trade paperback $9.95
   This book includes documentary source material not available in *The Current Justification Controversy*, an essay tracing the origins and continuation of this controversy throughout American Presbyterian churches, and an essay on the New Perspective on Paul by Robert L. Reymond.

Cornelius Van Til: The Man and The Myth
John W. Robbins   Trade paperback $2.45
   The actual teachings of this eminent Philadelphia theologian have been obscured by the myths that surround him. This book penetrates those myths and criticizes Van Til's surprisingly unorthodox views of God and the Bible.

The Current Justification Controversy
O. Palmer Robertson   Trade paperback $9.95
   From 1975 to 1982 a controversy over justification raged within Westminster Theological Seminary and the Philadelphia Presbytery of the Orthodox Presbyterian Church. As a member of the faculties of both Westminster and Covenant Seminaries during this period, O. Palmer Robertson was an important participant in this controversy. This is his account of the controversy, vital background for understanding the defection from the Gospel that is now widespread in Presbyterian churches.

God and Evil

The Everlasting Righteousness
Horatius Bonar   Trade paperback $8.95

   Originally published in 1874, the language of Bonar's masterpiece on justification by faith alone has been updated and Americanized for easy reading and clear understanding. This is one of the best books ever written on justification.

God and Evil: The Problem Solved
Gordon H. Clark   Trade paperback $5.95

   This volume is Chapter 5 of *Religion, Reason and Revelation,* in which Dr. Clark presents his solution to the problem of evil.

God-Breathed: The Divine Inspiration of the Bible
Louis Gaussen   Trade paperback $16.95

   Gaussen, a nineteenth-century Swiss Reformed pastor, comments on hundreds of passages in which the Bible claims to be the Word of God. This is a massive defense of the doctrine of the plenary and verbal inspiration of Scripture.

God's Hammer: The Bible and Its Critics
Gordon H. Clark   Trade paperback $10.95

   The starting point of Christianity, the doctrine on which all other doctrines depend, is "The Bible alone, and the Bible in its entirety, is the Word of God written, and, therefore, inerrant in the autographs." Over the centuries the opponents of Christianity, with Satanic shrewdness, have concentrated their attacks on the truthfulness and completeness of the Bible. In the twentieth century the attack was not so much in the fields of history and archaeology as in philosophy. Dr. Clark's brilliant defense of the complete truthfulness of the Bible is captured in this collection of eleven major essays.

The Holy Spirit
Gordon H. Clark   Trade paperback $8.95

   This discussion of the third person of the Trinity is both concise and exact. Dr. Clark includes chapters on the work of the Spirit, sanctification, and Pentecostalism. This book is part of his multi-volume systematic theology that began appearing in print in 1985.

The Incarnation
Gordon H. Clark   Trade paperback $8.95

   Who is Christ? The attack on the doctrine of the Incarnation in the nineteenth and twentieth centuries was vigorous, but the orthodox response was lame. Dr. Clark reconstructs the doctrine of the Incarnation, building and improving upon the Chalcedonian definition.

The Johannine Logos
Gordon H. Clark   Trade paperback $5.95

   Dr. Clark analyzes the relationship between Christ, who is the truth, and the Bible. He explains why John used the same word to refer to both Christ and his teaching. Chapters deal with the Prologue to John's Gospel; *Logos* and *Rheemata*; Truth; and Saving Faith.

Justification by Faith Alone
Charles Hodge   Trade paperback $10.95

    Charles Hodge of Princeton Seminary was the best American theologian of the nineteenth century. Here, for the first time, are his two major essays on justification in one volume. This book is essential in defending the faith.

Karl Barth's Theological Method
Gordon H. Clark   Trade paperback $18.95

    Karl Barth's Theological Method is perhaps the best critique of the Neo-orthodox theologian Karl Barth ever written. Dr. Clark discusses Barth's view of revelation, language, and Scripture, focusing on his method of writing theology, rather than presenting a comprehensive analysis of the details of Barth's theology.

Logical Criticisms of Textual Criticism
Gordon H. Clark   Trade paperback $3.25

    Dr. Clark's acute mind enables him to demonstrate the inconsistencies, assumptions, and flights of fancy that characterize the science of New Testament criticism.

Predestination
Gordon H. Clark   Trade paperback $10.95

    Dr. Clark thoroughly discusses one of the most controversial and pervasive doctrines of the Bible: that God is, quite literally, Almighty. Free will, the origin of evil, God's omniscience, creation, and the new birth are all presented within a Scriptural framework. The objections of those who do not believe in Almighty God are considered and refuted. This edition also contains the text of the booklet, *Predestination in the Old Testament*.

Sanctification
Gordon H. Clark   Trade paperback $8.95

    In this book, which is part of Dr. Clark's multi-volume systematic theology, he discusses historical theories of sanctification, the sacraments, and the Biblical doctrine of sanctification.

Study Guide to the Westminster Confession
W. Gary Crampton   Oversize paperback $10.95

    This *Study Guide* can be used by individuals or classes. It contains a paragraph-by-paragraph summary of the *Westminster Confession,* and questions for the student to answer. Space for answers is provided. The *Guide* will be most beneficial when used in conjunction with Dr. Clark's *What Do Presbyterians Believe?*

A Theology of the Holy Spirit
Frederick Dale Bruner   Trade paperback $16.95

    First published in 1970, this book has been hailed by reviewers as "thorough," "fair," "comprehensive," "devastating," "the most significant book on the Holy Spirit," and "scholarly." Gordon Clark described this book in his own book *The Holy Spirit* as "a masterly and exceedingly well researched exposition of Pentecostalism. The documentation is superb, as is also his penetrating analysis of their non-scriptural and sometimes contradictory conclusions." Unfortunately, the book is marred by the author's sacramentarianism.

The Trinity
Gordon H. Clark   Trade paperback $8.95

   Apart from the doctrine of Scripture, no teaching of the Bible is more fundamental than the doctrine of God. Dr. Clark's defense of the orthodox doctrine of the Trinity is a principal portion of his systematic theology. There are chapters on the Deity of Christ; Augustine; the Incomprehensibility of God; Bavinck and Van Til; and the Holy Spirit; among others.

What Calvin Says
W. Gary Crampton   Trade paperback $10.95

   This is a clear, readable, and thorough introduction to the theology of John Calvin.

What Do Presbyterians Believe?
Gordon H. Clark   Trade paperback $10.95

   This classic is the best commentary on the *Westminster Confession of Faith* ever written.

What Is Saving Faith?
Gordon H. Clark   Trade paperback $12.95

   This is the combined edition of *Faith and Saving Faith* and *The Johannine Logos*. The views of the Roman Catholic Church, John Calvin, Thomas Manton, John Owen, Charles Hodge, and B. B. Warfield are discussed in this book. Is the object of faith a person or a proposition? Is faith more than belief? Is belief thinking with assent, as Augustine said? In a world chaotic with differing views of faith, Dr. Clark clearly explains the Biblical view of faith and saving faith.

   In *The Johannine Logos*, Dr. Clark analyzes the relationship between Christ, who is the truth, and the Bible. He explains why John used the same word to refer to both Christ and his teaching. Chapters deal with the Prologue to John's Gospel; *Logos* and *Rheemata;* Truth; and Saving Faith.

Clark's Commentaries on the New Testament

Colossians	Trade paperback	$6.95
Ephesians	Trade paperback	$8.95
First Corinthians	Trade paperback	$10.95
First John	Trade paperback	$10.95
First and Second Thessalonians	Trade paperback	$5.95
New Heavens, New Earth (*First* and *Second Peter*)	Trade paperback	$10.95
The Pastoral Epistles (*1* and *2 Timothy* and *Titus*)	Hardback	$29.95
	Trade paperback	$14.95
Philippians	Trade paperback	$9.95

   All of Clark's commentaries are expository, not technical, and are written for the Christian layman. His purpose is to explain the text clearly and accurately so that the Word of God will be thoroughly known by every Christian.

The Trinity Library

We will send you one copy of each of the 58 books listed above for $500 (retail value $800), postpaid to any address in the U.S. You may also order the books you want individually on the order form on the next page. Because some of the books are in short supply, we must reserve the right to substitute others of equal or greater value in The Trinity Library. This special offer expires October 31, 2006.

Order Form

NAME _____

ADDRESS _____

_____

TELEPHONE _____

E-MAIL _____

Please:

❏ add my name to the mailing list for *The Trinity Review.* I understand that there is no charge for single copies of *The Review* sent to U.S. addresses.

❏ accept my tax deductible contribution of $ _____ .

❏ send me _____ copies of *God and Evil*. I enclose as payment U.S. $ _____ .

❏ send me The Trinity Foundation Library of 58 books. I enclose U.S. $500 as full payment.

❏ send me the following books. I enclose full payment in the amount of U.S. $ _____ for them.

_____

_____

_____

_____

The Trinity Foundation
Post Office Box 68
Unicoi, Tennessee 37692
Website: http://www.trinityfoundation.org/
United States of America

Shipping: Please add $6.00 for the first book, and 50 cents for each additional book. For foreign orders, please add $1.00 for each additional book.